AMERICAN ADVENTURES
Elementary

Student Book Part A

Ben Wetz

OXFORD
UNIVERSITY PRESS

eading and stening	Speaking and Functions	Writing	Pronunciation and Study skills
Free time Time at home The time of your life	• Asking about free time	• My free time: *also*	• /ɪz/ • Study habits
Communication quiz Cell phones Living language	• Doing a questionnaire • Asking for help with English	• An essay: periods and capital letters	• Word stress

• Culture File: Houses and homes   • World of Pop 1: Roxette, *Spending my time*

Winners A competition Soccer, soccer	• Asking about a prize	• A biography: time expressions	• /ɪd/, /t/, and /d/ • Remembering vocabulary
Volcano Lightning Tornado	• Talking about activities in the past	• A story: stages of writing	• /ɪŋ/

• Culture File: Teenagers and money   • World of Pop 2: Travis, *Why does it always rain on me?*

OXFORD
UNIVERSITY PRESS

Great Clarendon Street, Oxford OX2 6DP

Oxford University Press is a department of the University of Oxford.
It furthers the University's objective of excellence in research, scholarship,
and education by publishing worldwide in

Oxford New York

Auckland Cape Town Dar es Salaam Hong Kong Karachi
Kuala Lumpur Madrid Melbourne Mexico City Nairobi
New Delhi Shanghai Taipei Toronto

With offices in

Argentina Austria Brazil Chile Czech Republic France Greece
Guatemala Hungary Italy Japan Poland Portugal Singapore
South Korea Switzerland Thailand Turkey Ukraine Vietnam

OXFORD and OXFORD ENGLISH are registered trade marks of
Oxford University Press in the UK and in certain other countries

ISBN: 978 0 19 452727 9

Printed in Spain by Orymu, S.A.

ACKNOWLEDGEMENTS

The publishers and author would like to thank the following teachers for their help in developing the course: Angelica Puelles, Luciana Hernández, María Cecilia Shecre, Silvia Stagnaro, Corina Arguimbau, Fabiana Siciliano, Silvia Luppi, Graciela Beatriz Salinas, María Amelia Alexandre de Cetro, María Beatriz de Benedet, Paola Santanera, Susana Elsa Sainz, María Laura Provvisionato, Viviana Ameijenda, Vanessa Schwarzbach, Virginia Lorena Alvarez, Juana Nicenboim, Adriana Toniolli, Alejandra Rouzeaut, Lorena Mollini, Verónica de la Encina, María Celia Baez, María del Rosario González, Pierina Gatani, Patricia Arriondo, Andriana Gil, Elizabeth Felix, Daniela Oliveira Guerra, Debora Schisler, Elisabeth Moreira S. Silva, Flavia Moreira Landucci, Sonia Maria Proença Cury, Nilce Chaud Albano, Patricia Rossi Julio, Fife MacDuff, Maria Zita Bierrench, Helena Gordon, Beth Rodrigues Roselli, Mária Lucia Gallina, Beatriz de Farias, Maria de Lourdes Genestreti, Margareth Perucci, Maria Alice Gonçalves Antunes

Student Book
Illustrations by: Nila Aye/New Division pp 8 (objects), 9, 11 (objects), 60 (musical instruments), 86 (book, house), 96, 100 (signs); Jonas Bergstrand/CIA pp 15, 20 (street scene), 29, 42 (ex 2), 53 (bed), 59, 78, 81, 83, 97 (illnesses), 108 (recycling); Brett Breckon pp 19, 37, 86 (equipment); Chris Brown pp 79, 85; Stefan Chabluk pp 36, 42 (weather); Ian Cunliffe p 39 (times); Nick Duffy pp 11 (graph), 33, 47, 97 (no smoking); Andrew Foley/Eastwing pp 8 (activities), 34, 56 (map), 100 (illnesses); Jason Ford p 64; Simon Gurr pp 102, 103 (objects); Andre Labrie p 12; Monica Laita pp 45, 57, 58, 60 (CDs), 89, 103 (photos); Bill Ledger p 39 (scare crow); Andy Parker pp 44, 49, 50, 54; Andy Peters pp 56 (friendly/unfriendly), 108 (party); Ian Saxton/New Division pp 7, 10, 46, 52, 53, 108 (objects); Simeon Stout p 20 (dachshund); Lucy Truman/ New Division pp 23, 26, 48, 67, 92, 111, 114; Richard Williams/Eastwing p 72

We would also like to thank the following for the permission to reproduce photographs in the Student Book: Alamy Images pp 6 (playing guitar/Lebrecht Music & Arts Photo Library), 21 (American house/Chris Pancewicz), 24 (American house/Chris Pancewicz), 24 (apartments/Allan Ivy), 24 (semi-detached/Arcaid), 24 (Vanderbilt Mansion/Wolfgang Kaehler) 27 (Fifa World Cup 2006/Popperfoto), 31 (friends/Janine Wiedel Photo Library), 71 (San Francisco/ImageState), 72 (New York/Dorling Kindersley), 77 (Catskill Mountains/Creatas), 109 (Union Station/Philip Scalia), 112 (heart

balloons/PhotoSpin Inc), 113 (astronaut/ImageState); Ancient Art & Architecture Collection pp 14 (Egyptian hieroglyphics), 101 (totem pole); Allsport pp 28 (medal), 32 (team), 33 (Rimet & trophy), 76 (stadium), 98 (bikes); Emily Andersen pp 6 (martial arts), 11 (shopping), 21 (girl), 22, 23, 30, 44, 45, 65 (girl & boys), 66, 67, 72 (Hannah & Kath), 87 (Dean), 88, 89, 106, 109 (Palmer family), 110, 111; Art Archive p 80; Steve Betts pp 5 (computer), 9, 11 (Jenny), 13 (note, code, thumb), 16, 17, 19 (girl), 43 (Greg), 47, 55, 69, 101 (sofa), 107 (containers); Gareth Boden pp 10, 101 (boxes); Bruce Coleman Collection pp 35 (tornado, storm), 36 (volcano), 41 (volcano), 82 (shark); Bubbles Photolibrary pp 5 (walking), 62 (Westlife); Camera Press pp 28 (Walt Disney), 91 (punks); Collections pp 71 (city/Liz Stares, statue/Yuri Lewinski, London/Simon Hazelgrove), 77, 101 (stained glass); Corbis p 5 (play guitar, exercise), 74 (Mexico City); EMPICS Sports Photo Agency pp 27 (celebrating GCSE results/Rui Vieira/PA), 33 (Michelle Akers), 62 (Destiny's Child/Debbie Van Story/ABACA), 62 (Westlife/suzan/allactiondigital.com), 78 (Jack Black/ Dennis Van Tine/ABACA), 78 (Jessica Simpson/Baxter/ABACA), 78 (Orlando Bloom/Paul Smith), 102 (Heath Ledger/Jean/allactiondigital.com); Environmental Picture Library p 104 (volcano); Frank Spooner/Katz pp 35 (volcano), 36, 76 (shark); Fotosearch p71 (Aerial view of town/Joe Sohm); Getty Images pp 5 (meet friends, football, computer game), 14 (underwater), 19 (Britain), 21 (Roxette/Christian Charisius/Reuters), 24 (Alaska/National Geographic), 24 (family/Jenny Acheson/Riser), 24 (family/John-Francis Bourke/Zefa), 25 (office workers/Blend Images/R-R), 26 (Roxette/Christian Charisius/Reuters), 29, 35 (flood/Carlo Allegri), 64 (guitar, saxophone, mike), 69 (student/Iconica/R-R), 72 (American street/Robert Harding World Imagery), 73, 98 (Chris, swimmers), 101 (metal arch); Greg Evans International p 25 (elderly couple); Hulton Getty pp 33 (Jules Rimet), 98 (man at gym/Fabio Cardoso/Zefa); Impact Photos p 6 (eating hamburgers/Bruce Stephens); William Ing/Hawaii Tribune-Herald p 36 (Michael Benson); International Association of Mouth and Foot Painters (IAMFP) p 94; J. Allan Cash p 18 (Choctaw); Jerrican pp 5 (shopping), 14 (Braille), 18 (English), 34 (girl & boy), 71 (skyscraper), 101 (origami); London Features International pp 109 (Westlife), 114 (Westlife); Magnum Photos pp 76 (cars); Mark Mason p 13 (fridge magnets), 102; Mary Evans Picture Library pp 87 (Beatles), 90 (Beatles); NHPA pp 6 (tarantula), 105; OSF p 75; OUP p13 (mobile phone/Photodisc); Panos Pictures p 18 (Arabic); Phillips p 50 (gadgets); Photodisc p 83 (business man); Photofusion pp 27 (certificate), 91 (hip hop/Mark Cambell); Pictor International pp 25 (boy on porch); Popperfoto p 28 (Nobel prize, LeAnn Shannon), 42; Powerstock/Superstock pp 6 (spider boy), 64 (drum), 74 (Paris); PunchStock pp5 (girls on computer/ Digital Vision), 13 (waving/PhotoAlto), 46 (currency/Corbis), 71 (autumn town/Design Pics); Retna Pictures pp 5 (stay in), 35 (blizzard), 43 (Travis), 48, 60, 61, 65 (young girls/Digital Vision), 82, 107 (recycling bins/Photodisc); Reuters Pictures pp27 (Lottery winner A Whittaker/John Sommers II), Rex Features pp 14 (wrist phone), 27 (Roger Federer/Ron C Angle/BEI), 28 (Sheryel Hanuman/Eric Miller), 28 (Mother Teresa, Roger Robar), 32 (World Cup), 34 (Damon & Affleck), 35 (earthquake), 41 (hurricane), 62 (Backstreet Boys/ Eckehard Schulz/Pool), 65 (Nelly Furtado/Sipa Press), 70 (Nelly Furtado/Sipa Press), 78 (Maria Sharapova/Ron Angle/BEI), 87 (Backstreet Boys), 92 (Backstreet Boys); 78 (Will Smith, Jennifer Aniston), 82 (rescue worker), 83 (soldier, miner), 95 (famous people),102 (Shakira/Gregory Pace/BEI);Tim Rice/University of Western Ontario p 95 (Simona); Robert Harding Picture Library pp 43 (shopping), 76 (aerial view), 82 (firefighter, motorcycle); Ronald Grant Archive pp 12, 90 (John Travolta); Scholastic p 84; SPL p 51; Sportcam.net p 98 (man running); Stockmarket pp 18 (Hindi, Chinese), 74 (Bangkok); Topham/Picturepoint pp 14 (Maoris), 28 (Oscar); TRIP/Art Directors pp 14 (Chinese), 35 (hurricane), 38, 41 (earthquake), 76 (Hollywood).

Workbook
llustrations by: Nila Aye/New Division pp 4 (crossword except 4), 18 (housework); Frederico Botana p 50 (band); Brett Breckon pp 13, 27, 30, 31, 36, 48, 54 (animals), 77; Chris Brown pp 29, 55, 58 (scary things), 62, 66; France Chaulet p 42 (Kelly & Harry); Ian Cunliffe p 4 (4); Andrew Foley/ Eastwing pp 4 (Amanda & Mike), 5 (table tennis), 10, 17, 21, 23 (boys), 39 (if), 50 (Lena, Tom), 60, 68, 82; Mark Harrison p 42 (performers), 43; Andre Labrie pp 5 (Helen & grandfather), 9, 19, 23 (excursions), 32, 35, 37 (will, won't), 54 (superlatives), 59 (dirty boy), 75 (acting), 83; Andrew Peters pp 6, 11, 18 (faces), 52, 58 (spider), 61, 64, 65, 75 (objects), 80, 81; Ian Saxton pp 20, 37 (poster), 70, 76; Anthony Williams pp 16, 29, 38, 39 (castle), 44, 45, 59 (horror stories), 74.

We would like to thank the following for permission to reproduce photographs n the Workbook: Alamy Images pp8 (Cape Cod/Ernst Wrba), 82 (recycling/Garry Gay); Ace Photo Agency pp 40 (Sally/John Guidi), 78; Gareth Boden p 82 (metal, boxes, glass, wood); Bubbles Photolibrary p 14; Collections pp 24 (Cambridge/John Beldom), 52 (London); Corbis p 40 (Simon); Getty Images pp 26, 27, 28 (volcano), 40 (Jenny), 63, 65, 69, 80, 82 (books/Yang Tan/Stone+); Mary Evans Picture Library p 25; Photofusion p 8 (Sue), 61, 72; Powerstock pp 22, 24 (Oxford); Retna Pictures pp 28 (Claire Ward/Reeson), 71; SPL pp 24 (Stephen Hawking/Rob Stepney), 33; Trip/Art Directors pp 7, 11, 52 (Tokyo), 55, 56, 68, 76.

Commissioned photography by: Emily Andersen, Steve Betts, Gareth Boden and Mark Mason

1 Time out

Take a look!

Find the pages where you:
- write about your free time.
- read about people's hobbies.
- complete a questionnaire about jobs at home.

Vocabulary

Activities

1 Match the words in the box with activities 1–9. Then listen and repeat.

> go shopping   play sports
> play computer games   meet friends
> stay in   play the guitar   exercise
> surf the Internet   go out

2 Where do you do the activities in exercise 1? Make a list of places.

the shopping mall

● VOCABULARY • PAGE 124

Reading

1 🎧 **Read and listen. Then match texts 1–4 with photos a–d.**

What do you do in your free time?

1 Tanya

I go out a lot. I like going to the movies, and I often go shopping with my friends. My brother Nathan doesn't go out much. We have a new computer at home, and he uses it a lot. He writes to people and surfs the Internet. I don't use the computer much.
I have a new guitar, and that's my hobby right now. My dad plays the guitar too: he plays and sings in a band. He's really good, and he practices every day. He teaches me songs sometimes, but I'm a bit lazy and I don't practice.

2 Pete

I have a tarantula called Wanda. I like spiders because they're interesting animals. They can live for 30 years! Wanda usually eats insects and worms.

3 Carl

I go out and meet my friends on weekends. We don't like shopping, but we often meet at our local shopping mall. We usually have lunch at a fast food restaurant.

4 Jenny

I play a lot of sports, and I really like martial arts. I go to taekwondo classes with my friend Nick on Mondays and Wednesdays. Our teacher has a black belt. He doesn't speak a lot, but he's very good.

a

b

c

d

2 **Read the texts again and answer the questions.**

1 Does Tanya go out a lot?

2 Does Nathan like computers?

3 What instrument does Tanya's dad play?

4 What does Wanda eat?

5 When does Carl meet his friends?

6 When do Jenny and Nick go to taekwondo classes?

Look!

have

I **have** a new guitar.

He **has** a black belt.

⬤ GRAMMAR • PAGE 115

Pronunciation

/ɪz/

3 🎧 **Listen and repeat.**

1 plays   2 writes   3 uses

4 🎧 **Listen and repeat. Which verbs have the sound /ɪz/ ?**

1 practices   2 sings   3 surfs   4 teaches

Exploring grammar

Simple present

5 **Complete the chart with *do*, *don't*, *does*, and *doesn't*. Check your answers on page 6.**

Affirmative

I go out.
He writes to people.

Negative

I (1) ...... practice.
He (2) ...... speak a lot.

Questions

When (3) ...... Carl meet his friends?
When (4) ...... Jenny and Nick go to classes?

⬤ GRAMMAR • PAGE 115

6 **Look at the texts on page 6. Correct the sentences.**

Tanya plays the violin. *She doesn't play the violin. She plays the guitar.*

1 Tanya goes shopping with her brother.
2 Wanda eats vegetables.
3 Carl meets his friends on Thursdays.
4 Carl and his friends meet at his house.
5 Jenny goes to karate classes.
6 Jenny and Nick go to taekwondo classes on Tuesdays.

7 **Complete the questions with *do* or *does*. Then look at the pictures of Nick and Jenny's things. Answer the questions.**

What magazine *does* Jenny read?
She reads Music Today.

1 What sports ...... Jenny and Nick play?
2 ...... they listen to music?
3 ...... they buy magazines?
4 What magazine ...... Nick read?
5 What language ...... Jenny study?

Nick's things

Jenny's things

8 🎧 **Put the words in order. Then listen and check.**

1 like? / What animals / you / do
2 meet / Where / your friends? / do / you
3 you / read? / What magazines / do
4 play? / do / What sports / you
5 every day? / you / Do / go out
6 the Internet? / you / Do / surf

Speaking

9 **Work in pairs. Ask and answer the questions in exercise 8.**

A: *What animals do you like?*
B: *I like cats.*

⬤ **Finished?**

Write sentences about your free time.
I eat a lot of pizza.
I surf the Internet every day.

Time at home

Vocabulary

Jobs at home

1 🎧 Match the phrases in the box with pictures 1–6. Then listen and check.

> make dinner   wash the dishes
> clean your room   make your bed
> take out the garbage   go shopping

> **Look!**
>
> **Verbs + -ing**
> I like mak**ing** dinner.
> I don't like wash**ing** the dishes.

2 Write sentences about the jobs in exercise 1. Use *like* and *don't like*.

I like cleaning my room.

● VOCABULARY • PAGE 124

Reading

3 Complete the questionnaire. Then check your score at the bottom of the page.

Are you a **saint** at home?

1 How often do you make your bed?
  a Never.   b Sometimes.   c Always.

2 How often do you clean your room?
  a Never.   b Not usually.   c Always.

3 How often do you go shopping with your parents?
  a Never.   b Sometimes.   c Usually.

4 How often do you make dinner?
  a Never.   b Sometimes.   c Always.

5 How often do you wash the dishes?
  a Never.   b Sometimes.   c Always.

6 How often do you take out the garbage?
  a Never.   b Sometimes.   c Usually.

Key:
- Score 0 points for each a answer.
- Score 1 point for each b answer.
- Score 2 points for each c answer.

Your score:
- 0–4 points. Not very good! Are your parents very tired?
- 5–8 points. Not bad. You have a good attitude!
- 9–12 points. Amazing! Your parents are very lucky.

Listening

4 🎧 **Guess Barry's answers to the questionnaire. Then listen and check.**

I think that he never makes his bed.

5 🎧 **Listen again. Are the sentences true or false?**

1 Barry always makes his bed.
2 Barry doesn't usually clean his room.
3 He usually goes shopping with his parents.
4 He never makes dinner.
5 He sometimes washes the dishes.
6 He usually takes out the garbage.

Look!

Spelling rules: third person -s

make – mak**es**   go – go**es**
wash – wash**es**   try – tr**ies**

● GRAMMAR • PAGES 115–116

Exploring grammar

Adverbs of frequency

6 Look at the questionnaire on page 8 and complete the adverbs of frequency.

How often do you make your bed?
(1) N _ v _ r.
Not usually.
(2) S _ m _ t _ m _ s.
(3) _ s _ a _ l _.
(4) _ l w _ y s.

● GRAMMAR • PAGE 116

7 Put adverbs of frequency in the sentences.

I *usually* clean my room.

1 I eat in a restaurant.
2 My father makes dinner.
3 I speak English at home.
4 My mother washes the dishes.
5 My friend helps me with my homework.
6 I listen to music.

Speaking

8 Make questions with *How often ...?* In pairs, ask and answer.

A: *How often do you* go to bed after midnight?

B: *Never.*

1 ... wear sneakers at school?
2 ... use a computer?
3 ... sing in the shower?
4 ... write letters?
5 ... eat in bed?
6 ... get up after ten o'clock in the morning?

Finished?

Guess things about the other people in your class.

I think that Monica usually sings in the shower.

The time of your life

Study skills

Study habits

1 Look at Daniel's study habits. Which are good ideas? Which are bad ideas?

My study habits

1 I usually check new vocabulary in the vocabulary pages.

2 I never study at home.

3 I always try to remember example sentences.

4 I don't ask the teacher for help.

5 I sometimes copy my friend's homework.

Daniel

2 Write three of your good study habits.

I usually ask the teacher for help.

Listening

3 Read about the radio program.

Tuesday 8:00 p.m. *The time of your life*

How many minutes are there in a life? If you live for 75 years, the total is approximately 40 million minutes. That's a lot of minutes. Where does the time go?

4 🎧 Guess the answers to the questions. Then listen and check.

In 75 years, approximately how much time do we spend ...

1 **sleeping?**
   a 15 years   b 25 years

2 **cooking and eating?**
   a 3 years   b 9 years

3 **shopping?**
   a 3 years   b 1 year

4 **watching TV?**
   a 3 years   b 10 years

Look!

Big numbers

100	one hundred
325	three hundred and twenty-five
1,000	one thousand
1,018	one thousand and eighteen
1,755	one thousand, seven hundred, and fifty-five
400,000	four hundred thousand
1,000,000	one million

Speaking

5 **Work in pairs. Ask and answer the questions.**

1 How many hours do you usually sleep a night?

2 Do you watch TV every day?

3 Do you spend a lot of time shopping?

4 What do you do when you go out with your friends?

5 How many hours do you spend at school every week?

Writing

Writing about free time: *also*

We use *also* when we are giving more information about something.

6 **Read about Jenny's free time. Answer the questions.**

1 What activities does she do at home?

2 What activities does she do when she goes out?

My free time

At home

When I'm at home, I usually read or listen to music. I also study at home, and I help my parents. I never use a computer at home. I usually sleep for eight hours.

Out with friends

When I go out with friends, we usually play sports. We do taekwondo. We also go shopping, and we sometimes go to the movies.

7 **Look at the text again. Put *also* in your answers to exercise 6.**

8 **Complete the rule.**

also comes **before** / **after** the verb.

9 **Make lists of the activities that you do at home, and the activities that you do when you are out.**

Activities at home	Activities when I'm out
play computer games	*go rollerblading*

10 **Write two paragraphs about your activities at home and your activities when you are out with friends. Use *also*.**

Finished?

Make a bar chart for a typical day in your life. Include six activities.

hours

10
8
6
4
2

Sleeping At school Out with friends Dance class Watching TV Eating

Progress Check 1

Activities

1 **Match parts 1–9 with parts a–i.**

1 d

1	go	**a**	Internet
2	play	**b**	ping
3	meet fri	**c**	in
4	stay	**d**	out
5	play the	**e**	ends
6	go shop	**f**	guitar
7	surf the	**g**	computer games
8	exer	**h**	sports
9	play	**i**	cise

Jobs at home

2 **Complete expressions 1–6 with the verbs in the box.**

> clean take out make wash go make

 **1** ... shopping

 **2** ... the dishes

 **3** ... your room

 **4** ... your bed

 **5** ... the garbage

 **6** ... dinner

Simple present

3 **Choose the correct words.**

Nick: Hiro, Akio, I **think** / **thinks** that your show is fantastic. How often (**1**) **do** / **does** you practice?

Hiro: We (**2**) **practice** / **practices** every day.

Nick: Where (**3**) **do** / **does** you live?

Akio: We (**4**) **live** / **lives** in Japan, but we (**5**) **travel** / **travels** a lot.

Nick: Do you have a good teacher?

Hiro: Yes, he's excellent. He (**6**) **don't** / **doesn't** teach other people.

Nick: (**7**) **Do** / **Does** he travel with you?

Akio: No, he's old now and he (**8**) **prefer** / **prefers** to stay at home.

Adverbs of frequency

4 **Look at the chart. Then write five sentences about Jenny and Mick.**

Jenny never goes biking.

	Jenny	Mick
go biking	never	sometimes
watch TV	sometimes	not usually
help at home	always	usually

2 Communicate

Take a look!

Find the pages where you:
- do a quiz about forms of communication.
- read about different languages.
- complete a questionnaire about teenagers and communication.

Vocabulary

Forms of communication

1 Look at the code. Find the English words for pictures 1–6.

2 🎧 Listen and check your answers.

VOCABULARY · PAGE 124

A = ☺ B = ♦ C = ≈ D = ■ E = ♥ F = ☑ G = ♎
H = ♓ I = ✔ J = ☐ K = ♦ L = ☹ M = ☒ N = ☐
O = ▼ P = O Q = ♈ R = ◎ S = ✳ T = ● U = ▲
V = → W = ☽ X = ✦ Y = ✚ Z = ♋

① ≈♥☹☹ O♓▼☐♥

② ☒♥✳✳☺♎♥

③ ≈▼■♥

Bye.

④ ☹☺☐♎▲☺♎♥

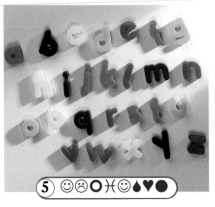

⑤ ☺☹O♓☺♦♥●

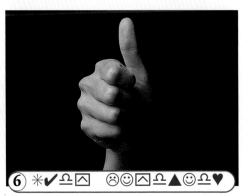

⑥ ✳✔♎☐ ☹☺☐♎▲☺♎♥

Communication quiz

Reading

1 **Do the quiz.**

1 What are these Maoris doing?
  a They're saying hello.
  b They're saying sorry.

2 This person is blind. She's reading with her fingers. What's the name of the special alphabet in her book?
  a Blind language.   **b** Braille.

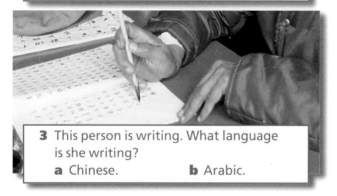

3 This person is writing. What language is she writing?
  a Chinese.   **b** Arabic.

4 This person is communicating with sign language. What's the message?
  a I'm OK.   **b** I have a problem.

5 This person is studying a very old text from Egypt. What's the name of the symbols?
  a Egyptian.   **b** Hieroglyphics.

6 What machine is this woman using?
  a A wrist phone.
  b A webcam.

2 🎧 **Listen and check your answers.**

Pronunciation

Word stress

3 🎧 **The words in the chart have the stress on the first syllable. Listen and repeat.**

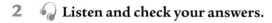

2 syllables	3 syllables
English	Arabic
letter	studying

4 🎧 **Add words 1–5 to the chart in exercise 3. Then listen and check.**

1 telephone
2 language
3 message
4 alphabet
5 special

Exploring grammar

Present continuous

5 **Look at the chart. How do we form the present continuous? Choose a or b.**

a With the verb *be* and an *-ing* form.

b With the verb *do* and an *-ing* form.

Affirmative

She's reading with her fingers.
They're saying hello.

Negative

She isn't writing Arabic.
They aren't saying sorry.

Questions

Is she writing Chinese?
What are these Maoris doing?

⦿ **GRAMMAR · PAGE 116**

6 **Read the quiz on page 14 again. Find another question and another affirmative sentence in the present continuous.**

7 **Put the words in order. Then answer the questions.**

Chinese? / Are / speaking / you

Are you speaking Chinese?

No, I'm not.

1 you / What language / are / writing?

2 talking / Are / on the phone? / you

3 What / is / doing? / your teacher

4 right now? / Are / studying / your classmates

5 wearing? / are / you / What

6 the person next to you / What / wearing? / is

7 you / Are / sleeping?

8 textbook / you / What / using? / are

8 **Look at the pictures and correct the sentences.**

He's listening to the teacher.

He isn't listening to the teacher. He's listening to music.

1 He's drawing a cat.

2 They're speaking Chinese.

3 She's writing a book.

4 They're reading a comic.

5 She's using a computer.

6 He's studying French.

◐ **Finished?**

Read the message. Then write a message for your partner. Use the code on page 13.

 Cell phones

Vocabulary

Verbs for communicating

1 🎧 **Check the meaning of the verbs. Then listen and repeat.**

1 e-mail	3 shout	5 talk	7 laugh
2 chat	4 argue	6 call	8 interrupt

⬤ VOCABULARY • PAGE 124

Reading

2 **Read opinions a–d. What do you think about cell phones?**

    a They're fantastic. I use a cell phone all the time.

    b I think they're good, but I don't have one.

    c I don't like cell phones.

    d I have a cell phone. I think they're useful sometimes.

3 **Read the texts. Match each person with one of the opinions in exercise 2.**

Cell phones

1 Lucy

I have a cell phone. I'm calling my mom now. I'm going home, but it's late and she's probably worried. I don't use my cell phone much, but I think they're useful. I don't argue with my parents when I'm late these days because I always call them. These days we argue about other things!

2 Mark

I think they're great. I use my cell phone all the time. I chat with my friends a lot, and we send text messages. I'm sending a text message to my girlfriend right now. My friend David can surf the Internet and send e-mails with his phone. Right now, he's looking for the basketball scores.

3 Jasmine

I think it's terrible when you're talking to a friend and suddenly their phone rings. It interrupts your conversation. And sometimes you're watching a movie at the theater and you hear a cell phone. Why do people need them? People can't have cell phones in class at my school. I think that's a good idea.

4 **Read the text again and answer the questions.**

    1 Is Lucy calling a friend?

    2 How often does Lucy use a cell phone?

    3 Does Lucy argue with her parents?

    4 How often does Mark use his cell phone?

    5 What is Mark sending to his girlfriend?

    6 What is David doing?

    7 Why doesn't Jasmine like cell phones?

    8 Do people use cell phones in Jasmine's class at school?

Exploring grammar

Simple present and present continuous

5 **Match examples a and b with rules 1 and 2.**

Examples

    a We argue about things.

    b I'm calling my mom.

Rules

    1 We use the simple present when we talk about habits and routines.

    2 We use the present continuous when we talk about actions in progress right now.

⬤ GRAMMAR • PAGE 116

6 Choose the correct form of the verbs.

David: What are you doing?

Lucy: Shh! (**1**) **I listen / I'm listening** to Mark. (**2**) **He talks / He's talking** to Clare.

David: And (**3**) **what does he say / what's he saying**?

Lucy: Well, (**4**) **he laughs / he's laughing** right now.

David: Is he Clare's boyfriend?

Lucy: I don't know, but (**5**) **they meet / they're meeting** after school every day.

David: Yes, and (**6**) **she usually helps / she's usually helping** him with his homework.

Lucy: Look! (**7**) **He shouts / He's shouting** at her now. Mmm. Very interesting!

7 Complete Mark and Clare's phone call.

Mark: Hi, Clare. It's Mark. Listen, I *'m calling* (call) from David's house. We (**1**) ...... (watch) a DVD. Do you want to come?

Clare: Oh, no! Thanks, but David always (**2**) ...... (watch) terrible DVDs.

Mark: Yeah, yeah! Come on, Clare.

Clare: No, I can't. I (**3**) ...... (study) right now.

Mark: Oh, Clare! You never (**4**) ...... (go out).

Clare: Hey! You (**5**) ...... (shout)!

Mark: I (**6**) ...... (not shout)! Listen, I have to go. See you tomorrow.

Clare: OK. Bye, Mark.

8 🎧 Listen and check your answers. Then practice the dialog in exercise 7.

9 Complete the questionnaire with the words in the box.

> do   call   calling   are   argue   arguing
> laugh   ~~laughing~~   ~~laugh~~   you

Questionnaire

Teenagers and communication

A Mark's *laughing*.
- Do you *laugh* a lot?
- What do you (**1**) ...... about?

B Lucy and her mother (**2**) ...... arguing. They're (**3**) ...... about Lucy's homework.
- Do you often (**4**) ...... with your parents?
- Why (**5**) ...... you argue?

C David's (**6**) ...... a friend.
- Do you often (**7**) ...... people?
- Who do (**8**) ...... call?

Speaking

10 Work in pairs. Ask and answer the questions in exercise 9.

◯ Finished?

Make words from the letters in COMMUNICATE.

can

Living language

Reading

1 🎧 **Read and listen. How many languages are mentioned in the text?**

Living language

Experts say that there are now about 6,000 languages in the world. The five with the most speakers are Mandarin Chinese, English, Spanish, Hindi, and Arabic. In total, almost one billion people speak Mandarin Chinese.

Some languages are dying. Experts think that over the next century more than half of the world's languages could die. Right now there are over 400 languages in serious danger of extinction. This means that only a few people are speaking the language.

Only a few thousand people now speak Choctaw, the language of the Choctaw Indians in North America. The Choctaw people are trying to preserve their language and traditions. Language classes are available in parts of the U.S., and you can also learn on the Internet!

Languages also change. When we communicate with people from other countries we learn new ideas and new words. In English, there are words from over 120 different languages. *Pizza* and *pasta*, for example, are Italian words, *mosquito* is a Spanish word, and *piranha* is from Brazilian Portuguese. People travel, and languages travel too!

Chinese

English

Hindi

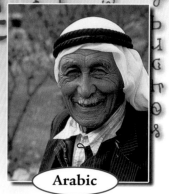

Arabic

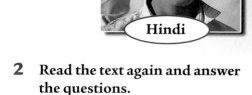

Choctaw

2 **Read the text again and answer the questions.**

1 How many different languages are there in the world?

2 How many people speak Mandarin Chinese?

3 How many languages could die over the next 100 years?

4 Do a lot of people speak Choctaw?

5 How are the Choctaw trying to preserve their language?

6 What language does the word *mosquito* come from?

Look!

Countries and nationalities

America – American

Brazil – Brazilian

Italy – Italian

Portugal – Portuguese

Spain – Spanish

Writing

An essay: periods and capital letters

3 Look at the text on page 18 again. Are these sentences true or false?

1 We start new sentences with a capital letter.

2 We end sentences with a period.

3 We do not use capital letters for the names of languages.

4 We use capital letters for the names of people and countries.

4 Rewrite the text with capital letters and periods.

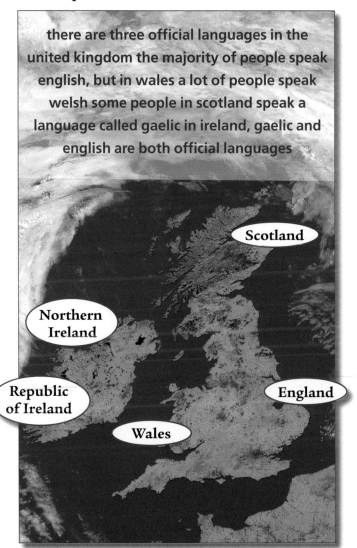

there are three official languages in the united kingdom the majority of people speak english, but in wales a lot of people speak welsh some people in scotland speak a language called gaelic in ireland, gaelic and english are both official languages

Scotland

Northern Ireland

Republic of Ireland

England

Wales

5 Write about languages in your country. Use the text in exercise 4 as a model.

Listening

6 🎧 Listen and answer the questions.

1 What is Bethan doing?

2 Does Bethan's grandmother speak Welsh?

3 How many words does Bethan teach Mark?

7 🎧 Listen again. Complete the sentences.

1 ...... "hello" in Welsh?

2 Sorry, can you ....?

3 How do you ...... "goodbye" in Welsh?

Speaking

8 🎧 Listen and repeat. Then test your partner. Take turns to look at the list.

A: How do you say "hello" in Choctaw?

B: Halito.

Common phrases in Choctaw

Choctaw	English
Halito.	Hello.
Chim achukma?	How are you?
Yokoke.	Thank you.
Binili.	Sit down.
Ant chukoa.	Come in.
A.	Yes.
Keyu.	No.

Finished?

Make anagrams with the names of languages. Then give them to your partner to work out.

sCihene – **Chinese**

Progress Check 2

Forms of communication

1 **Complete the words.**

1 s _ g _
2 _ e s _ _ g _
3 c _ d _
4 a _ p _ a b _ _
5 l _ n _ _ a _ e
6 c _ ll ph _ n _

Verbs for communicating

2  **Listen and match situations 1–5 with sentences a–e.**

a She's laughing.
b It's talking.
c She's calling a friend.
d They're arguing.
e He's shouting.

Present continuous

3 **Write questions about the picture. Then write the answers.**

What – Andy – do?
What is Andy doing?
He's listening to music.

1 Beth – shout?
2 What Kim – eat?
3 Kim and Sally – argue?
4 Andy – listen to Beth?
5 What Dave – do?

Simple present and present continuous

4 **Complete the rules.**

1 We use the ...... when we talk about actions in progress now.
2 We use the ...... when we talk about habits and routines.

5 **Choose the correct form of the verbs.**

What **do you do / are you doing**?

(1) **I laugh / I'm laughing.**

Why (2) **do you laugh / are you laughing**?

Look at that dog!

That's Joe's dog. (3) **He goes / He's going** for a walk every day.

People never (4) **laugh / are laughing** at Joe.

20

The World of English 1

Friends and Neighbors
(pages 22 and 23)

Review: **simple present and present continuous**

Function: **Making requests**

1 What's this girl's name?

Culture File
(pages 24 and 25)

Topic: **Houses and homes**

2 What kind of house is this?

The World of Pop
(page 26)

Artist: **Roxette**

Country: **Sweden**

Song: **Spending my time**

3 When is Marie's birthday?

Friends and Neighbors

Let's make a deal

1

Dad	Luke, can you wash the dishes, please?
Luke	Oh Dad, I always wash the dishes. Isn't it Nikki's turn?
Dad	OK, where is she? NIKKI! I suppose she's talking to that guy again. What's his name?
Nikki	Dad, I'm here. And this is Greg, you know ... our neighbor.
Dad	Oh ... ah ... yes, hi there, Greg.

2

Greg	Nikki, can you help me with my math homework?
Nikki	Why? What's the problem?
Greg	I don't understand it.
Nikki	I'm kind of busy, but OK. I suppose so.
Greg	Great, thanks.

3 **Teacher** Nikki Palmer, are you listening? Can I see you after class, please?

4

Nikki	What on earth are you doing here?
Greg	Look! I got a B+ on that math homework. Can you help me again?
Nikki	I don't know. I'm in trouble now, and it's your fault.
Greg	Oh, come on, Nikki, please.
Nikki	Mmm. OK. I have an idea. Let's make a deal.

5

Dad	Oh, hi there, Greg. Why are you washing our dishes? Nikki, what's going on here?
Nikki	Don't worry, Dad. It's the magic of mathematics!

Reading

1 🎧 **Read and listen to Friends and Neighbors. Then answer the questions.**

1. What are the names of the teenagers in the story?
2. Whose turn is it to wash the dishes?
3. Why does Greg need help with his math homework?
4. Why does the teacher speak to Nikki?
5. Why is Greg washing the dishes?

Useful expressions

2 **Find the expressions in the story. Then check their meaning.**

1. I'm kind of busy.
2. It's your fault.
3. Let's make a deal.
4. Don't worry.

Dialog

Making requests

3 🎧 **Look at this extract from Friends and Neighbors. Listen and repeat. Concentrate on your rhythm and intonation.**

A: Nikki, can you help me with my math homework?

B: Why? What's the problem?

A: I don't understand it.

B: I'm kind of busy, but OK. I suppose so.

A: Great, thanks.

4 **Look at the situations in the pictures. Then think of answers for questions 1–4.**

1. You want to borrow a friend's cell phone. Why?
2. You want to use a friend's bike. Why?
3. You need some money. Why?
4. You need some help. Why?

5 **Practice a dialog in pairs. Change the blue words in the dialog in exercise 3. Use your ideas from exercise 4.**

Culture File 1

Houses and homes

1 What are your impressions of American houses from books or movies?

2 Match photos 1–6 with descriptions a–f.

a **A duplex** is one of a symmetrical pair of joined houses. *4*

b **A single-family house** is separate from other houses and has a yard all around it.

c **An apartment** is a set of rooms where people live in a tall building.

d **A bungalow** is a house on one floor.

e **A cottage** is a small house outside of the city that is for vacations or weekends.

f **A mansion** is a very large house with lots of rooms and land around it.

Lynn, David, Claire, and Callum Stonehouse

Our house is a duplex from the 1930s. There are three bedrooms so my sister and I can have a bedroom each. We also have a garage and back yard. It's not far from downtown, and I can walk to school. My best friend lives in a single-family house and his room is huge! His house also has a TV and game room!

Jamie, Elizabeth, and Harriet Chilford

We inherited our house when Jamie's father died three years ago. It's an old mansion from the 19th century. It's beautiful, but it can be a lot of work. There are ten bedrooms, five reception rooms, and six bathrooms! It's also an expensive house. We have a cleaning crew, a gardener, and a full-time housekeeper. The heating costs are also very high. The winters are very cold here. Sometimes we dream about a nice three bedroom apartment in New York City.

3 Look at photos 1–4 and guess which type of house in exercise 2 the people live in. Then read the texts and check your answers.

4 Read the texts and complete the chart.

Present house	Date built	Location	Ideal house
1 Duplex			
2 Mansion			
3 Apartment			
4 Bungalow			

Charlotte and Andrew Roberts

I rented this apartment in 2005. It was new then. Andrew moved in when we got married. It's small – it only has one bedroom. When people stay, they sleep on the sofa bed in the living room! However, it's very easy to clean and very near the subway station. Andrew wants to buy a house. Houses are very expensive in the city, but there are some nice duplexes near us. He's right. Our place really is very small.

George and Madge Carter

George and I always wanted to live by the ocean. We moved to this house when I retired last year. It was built in the 1950s. It's ideal for us because George has a bad leg, and it doesn't have any stairs. It's also has a small yard that we enjoy looking after. It really is our dream house – we can walk to the beach in five minutes.

5 🎧 **Jack is showing his English friend, Neil, around his house. Listen and number the parts of the house in the order they are mentioned.**

a kitchen
b office
c living room
d front yard *1*
e back yard
f porch
g bedrooms
h dining room
i bathrooms
j garage

6 🎧 **Listen again. Match the two halves of the sentences.**

1 The porch   a has a computer and a TV.

2 The house   b are upstairs.

3 The office   c has an en-suite bathroom.

4 Jack's room   d has a swing seat.
5 The five bedrooms   e has air-conditioning.
6 Neil's room   f is downstairs.

7 Complete the table with the words in the box.

> yard   ~~office~~   garage
> kitchen   bedroom   porch

Inside the house	Outside the house
office	....
....	....
....	....

Project

Make a poster about the different types of houses in your country. Think about:

• What different types of houses are there?
• Where do you live?
• What is your dream home?

Add pictures to your poster.

The World of Pop 1

Per

Full name: Per-Hakan Gessle

Born: Sweden, January 12th, 1959

Hobbies: reading, tennis, collecting records

Likes: guitars

Marie

Full name: Gun-Marie Fredriksson

Born: Sweden, May 30th, 1958

Hobbies: listening to classical music, playing ice hockey, jogging

Likes: pasta

Roxette (Sweden)

1 **Read the information about Roxette and answer the questions.**

1 How old is Per Gessle?

2 Are Per and Marie from Sweden?

3 What are Per's hobbies?

4 What's Marie's favorite food?

2 🎧 **Complete the song with the words in the box. Then listen and check.**

> sky ~~time~~ kiss you call read
> missing think get up

3 **Write true or false for sentences 1–6.**

1 She's interested in the TV.

2 She's interested in her book.

3 She misses her boyfriend.

4 She calls her boyfriend.

5 She speaks to him on the phone.

6 She feels good.

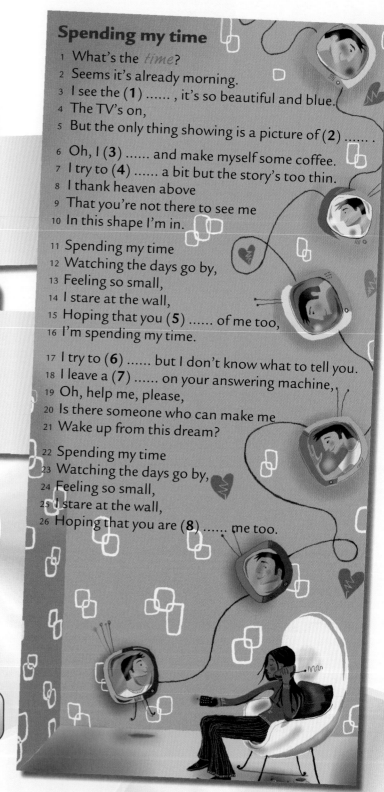

Spending my time

1 What's the *time*?
2 Seems it's already morning.
3 I see the (**1**) ...... , it's so beautiful and blue.
4 The TV's on,
5 But the only thing showing is a picture of (**2**) ......

6 Oh, I (**3**) ...... and make myself some coffee.
7 I try to (**4**) ...... a bit but the story's too thin.
8 I thank heaven above
9 That you're not there to see me
10 In this shape I'm in.

11 Spending my time
12 Watching the days go by,
13 Feeling so small,
14 I stare at the wall,
15 Hoping that you (**5**) ...... of me too,
16 I'm spending my time.

17 I try to (**6**) ...... but I don't know what to tell you.
18 I leave a (**7**) ...... on your answering machine,
19 Oh, help me, please,
20 Is there someone who can make me
21 Wake up from this dream?

22 Spending my time
23 Watching the days go by,
24 Feeling so small,
25 I stare at the wall,
26 Hoping that you are (**8**) ...... me too.

3 Prizes

Take a look!

Find the pages where you:
- listen to a story about a competition in a magazine.
- read about the World Cup.
- read about four prize winners.

Vocabulary

Prizes

1 Match the prizes with photos 1–5. Then listen and repeat.

> medal   certificate   cup   check   trophy

2 What Olympic sports do you know? Make a list.

Swimming, ...

VOCABULARY • PAGE 124

Reading

1 🎧 **Complete the texts with the numbers in the box. Then listen and check.**

> 41.45   26   1910   200   13   1923

LeAnn Shannon

Olympic gold medallist

In the 1996 Paralympic Games, LeAnn Shannon won gold medals for the 100, (1) ......, and 400 meters. She was (2) ...... years old. Then in 1998 she beat the U.S. national record for the 200, 400, and 800 meters.

Nobel Prize winner

Mother Teresa of Calcutta was born in Macedonia in (3) .... She didn't stay in Macedonia. She went to India and helped the poor. She worked in India for the rest of her life. In 1979 she won the Nobel Peace Prize for her work. She died in 1997.

Mother Teresa

Oscar winner

Walt Disney and his brother started the Disney movie studios in (4) .... Some of their famous movies were Pinocchio, Dumbo, and Snow White. Walt also created Mickey Mouse and Disneyland. When he died, he had (5) ...... Oscars.

Walt Disney

Sheryel Hanuman

Millionaire

This is Sheryel Hanuman's check for (6) ...... million dollars. When Sheryel won the money, she didn't go on one vacation, she went on several vacations. She also bought a car and a house, and she gave a lot of money to friends and family.

2 **Read the texts again. Are the sentences true or false?**

1 LeAnn Shannon won the 800 meters.

2 Mother Teresa stayed in Macedonia.

3 Mother Teresa won the Nobel Peace Prize in 1997.

4 Walt Disney didn't have a brother.

5 Walt Disney didn't win any Oscars.

6 Sheryel Hanuman helped people with her money.

Pronunciation

Simple past: /ɪd/, /t/, and /d/

3 🎧 **Listen and repeat.**

    1 created /ɪd/   **2** helped /t/   **3** died /d/

4 🎧 **Listen and repeat. Which verb ends with the sound /ɪd/?**

    1 stayed   **2** started   **3** worked

⬤ GRAMMAR · PAGE 117

Exploring grammar

Simple past: affirmative and negative

5 **Look at the examples. Then complete the rules with *negative*, *regular*, and *irregular*.**

Regular verbs	
Affirmative	**Negative**
She **helped**.	He **didn't help**.
She **stayed**.	He **didn't stay**.
Irregular verbs	
Affirmative	**Negative**
He **won**.	She **didn't win**.
He **bought** a car.	She **didn't buy** a house.

Rules

The past forms of (1) ...... verbs end in **-ed**.
The past forms of (2) ...... verbs are all different.
The past (3) ...... form is **didn't + infinitive**.

⬤ GRAMMAR · PAGE 117

Vocabulary

Irregular verbs

6 **Write the simple past of the verbs.**

    1 go   **3** have   **5** do   **7** become

    2 give   **4** meet   **6** get up   **8** see

⬤ IRREGULAR VERBS · INSIDE BACK COVER

7 **Complete the text with the verbs in the box.**

did   ~~got up~~   went   had   went   met

Diary of a teenage champion

Yesterday I *got up* at 4:30 in the morning. I (**1**) ...... breakfast, and then I (**2**) ...... to the gym. I trained for three hours before school. After school, I (**3**) ...... a friend and we trained for two hours at the swimming pool. I (**4**) ...... my homework at eight o'clock, and I (**5**) ...... to bed at nine o'clock.

8 **Write about your day yesterday.**

Yesterday I got up at ...

9 **Complete the sentences with the correct form of the simple past.**

Fortunate Fred's day

    1 He ...... (get up) at 6:30.

    2 He ...... (go) to work.

    3 He ...... (listen) to his boss all day.

    4 After work, he ...... (meet) his wife.

    5 They ...... (have) dinner in a burger bar.

    6 He ...... (buy) a lottery ticket.

    7 He ...... (give) his wife a rose.

10 **Fortunate Fred won the lottery! The next day he was a millionaire. Write negative and affirmative sentences about his day.**

He didn't get up at 6:30.
He got up at 11:30.

⬤ **Finished?**

Imagine you are a millionaire. Write your shopping list.

Two helicopters, ...

A competition

Listening

1 🎧 **Put photos a–e in order. Then listen and check .**

1 b

SATURDAY MORNING……

Oh! No, I didn't. It was in my bag, but I forgot.

Look! There's a competition in this magazine. You can win tickets for the World Cup.

Competition
Sports Magazine
New York NY 10016

Did you answer the questions?

Yes, I did. They weren't difficult.

TWO WEEKS LATER …

Mom, can you mail this, please?

2   Answer the questions.

1 What did Corey buy?

2 What was the prize for the competition?

3 Did Corey's mother take the letter?

4 Did Corey win the competition?

5 Did his mother mail the letter?

6 Did he shout at his mother?

Exploring grammar

Simple past: questions

3 Complete the chart with *did* and *didn't*.

Questions		
Did	you	answer the questions?
(**1**)	you	mail my letter?
Short answers		
Yes,	I	(**2**) ....
No,	I	(**3**) ....

(**GRAMMAR** • PAGE 117)

4 🎧 **Complete the dialog. Then listen and check.**

Emily: Hey, Josh! I won a competition.

Josh: Really? What *did you* win?

Emily: I won tickets for the Grand Prix.

Josh: Awesome! How many tickets (**1**) ...... win?

Emily: Two.

Josh: Who (**2**) ...... go with?

Emily: I went with Danny.

Josh: (**3**) ...... have a good time?

Emily: Yes, we (**4**) .... It was fantastic.

Josh: (**5**) ...... meet the stars?

Emily: Yes, I (**6**) .... I got five autographs.

Josh: And (**7**) ...... buy any presents?

Emily: No, I (**8**) .... Sorry, Josh!

5 **Look at the "Dream Ticket" competition. Write questions to ask the winner.**

What did you win?

The Dream Ticket competition

WIN TICKETS TO ONE OF THESE FAMOUS SPORTS EVENTS!

The World Cup	A Grand Prix	The Olympic games
	The NBA finals	

Speaking

6 **Work in pairs. Ask and answer the questions from exercise 5.**

A: *What did you win?*
B: *I won tickets to ...*

was / were

7 **Look at page 30 and complete the examples.**

It *was* in my bag.
They (**1**) ...... difficult.
What (**2**) ...... the prize?

(**GRAMMAR** • PAGE 118)

8 **Complete the questions with *was* and *were*. Then write the answers.**

When *was* the first Grand Prix? (1906)
The first Grand Prix was in 1906.

1 Who ...... the Formula 1 champion in 2006? (Fernando Alonso)

2 Where ...... the first Olympics? (Greece)

3 When ...... beach volleyball first an Olympic sport? (2000)

4 Who ...... the winners of the World Cup in 1958, 1962, 1970, 1994, and 2002? (Brazil)

Finished?

Write about a perfect prize. Where did you go? What did you see, buy, and eat?
I went to the Olympics.

Soccer, soccer

Listening

1 🎧 Guess the answers to the quiz questions. Then listen and check.

World Cup Quiz

1 **When and where was the first World Cup tournament?**

  a **Brazil in 1950.**

  b **Uruguay in 1930.**

2 **How many European teams were in the tournament?**

  a **Ten.**

  b **Four.**

3 **How did the teams travel from Europe?**

  a **By boat.**

  b **By plane.**

4 **Why didn't some teams go to the tournament?**

  a **They didn't have time or money.**

  b **A war started.**

5 **Who were the winners?**

  a **Brazil.**

  b **Uruguay.**

The winners of the first World Cup.

Study skills

Remembering vocabulary

2 Read the ideas for remembering vocabulary. Do you have any other ideas?

  1 Draw a picture of the word.

  2 If the new word is a verb, write the present and the past forms.

  3 Copy the word in a sentence or invent an example sentence.

> tournament =
> The World Cup is a tournament.
>
> start – started =
> I start school at 8:30.
>
> winners =
> Italy were the winners of the World Cup in 2006.

3 Write words 1–5 in your vocabulary notebook. Use ideas from exercise 2 to help you to remember them.

  1 travel   4 money

  2 team   5 war

  3 boat

Reading

4 Read the text about Jules Rimet on page 33. Check the meaning of any new words.

5 Read the text again and answer the questions.

  1 Where was Jules Rimet from?

  2 Did he play soccer at school and in university?

  3 What did he do after university?

  4 What idea did he have after World War One?

  5 When did he become president of FIFA?

  6 How did FIFA commemorate Jules Rimet's work?

Jules Rimet
Founder of the World Cup

Jules Rimet (on the left in the picture) was born in France in 1873. At school and in university, he was an excellent student. He liked sports, but he never played soccer. He preferred field and track.

After university, he worked in business and for charities. Then, in 1914, he went to fight in World War One. After his experiences in the war, he became a pacifist and had the idea for an international soccer tournament.

In 1921, he became president of the Federation of International Football Associations (FIFA), and three years later he invited different nations to participate in the first World Cup. Thirteen teams played in the first tournament in 1930.

In 1946, FIFA named the trophy the Jules Rimet World Cup, to commemorate his 25 years as president. Jules Rimet died in 1956.

football (U.K.) = soccer (U.S.)

Writing

A biography: time expressions

6 Complete the sentences with expressions from the text.

1 Jules Rimet was born in France ....

2 .... he worked in business.

3 ...... in 1914 he went to fight in the World War One.

4 .... he invited different nations to the first World Cup.

7 Read the sentences about Michelle Akers. Put them in order.

a In 1985, she played on the U.S. national team.

b In 1991, her women's team became the FIFA Women's World Champions.

c Michelle Akers started playing soccer in 1978. She went to university in 1984.

d In 1996, she won a gold medal at the Olympics.

e In 2000, she became FIFA's Woman Player of the Century.

8 Write about Michelle Akers. Use the sentences in exercise 7 and *After*, *Then*, and ... *years later*.

Finished?

Draw a ticket for a sports tournament. Include information about the prize, date, time, and price.

Progress Check 3

Prizes

1 Find five types of prizes in the word spiral.

1 medal

Irregular verbs

2 Write the infinitive of verbs 1–9.

1	did	**4**	got up	**7**	bought
2	went	**5**	gave	**8**	saw
3	had	**6**	met	**9**	won

Simple past: affirmative and negative

3 Complete the text with the correct form of the simple past.

Friends win prizes

When Matt Damon and Ben Affleck were young, they *lived* (live) in the same city and they (**1**) ...... (meet) at school. They soon became friends, and they both (**2**) ...... (act) in drama groups. They (**3**) ...... (study) at university, but they (**4**) ...... (not stop) acting. At first they (**5**) ...... (not act) in the same movies, but they were both in *Good Will Hunting*. They also (**6**) ...... (write) the movie, and they (**7**) ...... (win) an Oscar for the story. They (**8**) ...... (not go) to the Oscar ceremony with their girlfriends – they went with their mothers.

Simple past: questions

4 Make questions in the simple past with the words in the circles. Then write your answers.

> *A: Did you go out on Friday evening?*
> *B: Yes, I did.*

study
go out
eat in a restaurant
meet friends
watch TV
go shopping

Friday
Saturday
Sunday

morning
afternoon
evening

?

was / were

5 Complete the dialog with *was, wasn't, were,* and *weren't.*

Joe: Hey, Tim. I *wasn't* here on the weekend. (**1**) ...... you at the game?

Tim: Yes, I (**2**) ....

Joe: (**3**) ...... it good?

Tim: No, it (**4**) .... The Knicks (**5**) ...... terrible. But I watched it again on TV, and I have it on video.

Joe: Why? (**6**) ...... the shots good?

Tim: No, they (**7**) .... But look! I (**8**) ...... on the program!

4 ○ The elements

Take a look!

Find the pages where you:
- read about a dangerous rescue.
- listen to a story about a tornado.
- read about lightning.

Vocabulary

Natural phenomena

1 🎧 **Match the words with photos 1–9. Then listen and check.**

> earthquake   volcano   hurricane
> blizzard   tornado   storm   flood
> lightning   drought

⬤ **VOCABULARY • PAGE 125**

2 **What weather adjectives can you remember? Make a list.**

windy, ...

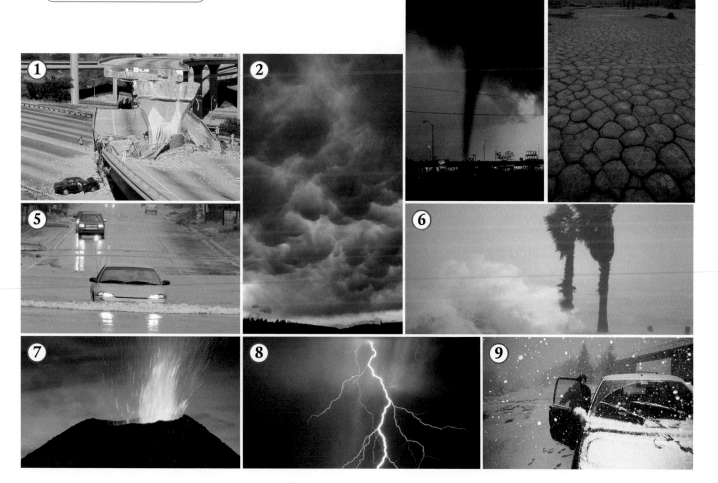

Reading

1 **Read the text. Put sentences a–e in order.**

   a Duddy and Hosking escaped from the volcano.

   b The helicopter crashed.

   c Duddy and Hosking contacted Hauptman.

   d Hauptman rescued Benson.

   e Benson and Duddy were filming the volcano.

2 **Read the text again and answer the questions.**

   1 What was Michael Benson's job?

   2 How did Hosking escape from the volcano?

   3 What did Benson drink in the volcano?

   4 How did Duddy and Hosking help Benson?

   5 What was the weather like the next day?

   6 How long was Benson in the volcano?

Exploring grammar

Past continuous: affirmative and negative

3 **Look at the rules and complete the chart.**

Rules
We use the past continuous when we describe the progress of an action in the past.
We form the past continuous with **was** and **were** and the **-ing** form of a verb.

I / He / She / It	(1) ...... / **wasn't** moving.
We / You / They	(2) ...... / **weren't** moving.

⬤ **GRAMMAR • PAGE 118**

4 **Find six examples of the past continuous in the text.**

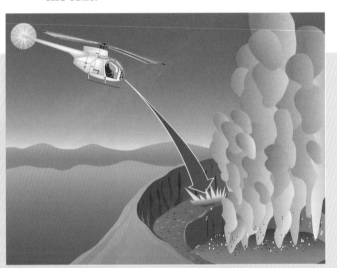

Rescue from the inferno

In November 1992 cameramen Michael Benson and Chris Duddy were in a helicopter, filming the Pu'u O'o volcano in Hawaii. The pilot, Craig Hosking, was flying over the volcano when the helicopter's engine stopped. The helicopter crashed into the crater. The three men escaped from the helicopter, but they were now inside the crater of an active volcano, only meters from the hot lava.

Duddy finally climbed out of the volcano and a second helicopter rescued Hosking. But Benson was in a very difficult position. He spent a night of agony inside the crater. Hot, acidic gas was coming from the volcano. Benson didn't have any food, but it was raining and he drank some rainwater.

Benson's colleagues were safe, but they weren't resting. They were trying to contact Tom Hauptman, an expert helicopter pilot.

The next day Hauptman flew to the volcano. The weather wasn't good. It was very cloudy, but the pilot saw Benson through the clouds. Benson was moving; he was alive!

Hauptman rescued Benson and flew to a hospital in Hawaii. Benson was sick, but he survived his 48 hours of torture in the volcano.

5 🎧 **Listen and choose the correct words.**

1 Tom **was** / **wasn't** watching a movie on TV.

2 People **were** / **weren't** shouting in the movie.

3 People **were** / **weren't** escaping from an earthquake.

4 People **were** / **weren't** escaping from a volcano.

5 Tom **was** / **wasn't** enjoying the movie.

6 Susan **was** / **wasn't** enjoying the movie.

Vocabulary

Verbs of movement

6 **Match the words and pictures 1–6.**

| climb   lift   fall   crash   fly   move |

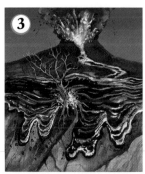 

7 **Complete the text with the correct form of the verbs. Use the past continuous.**

Five kilometers from here the volcano *was erupting* (erupt). There was a lot of confusion. People (**1**) ...... (run) and shouting, but I (**2**) ...... (not move). I (**3**) ...... (watch) the volcano. Rocks (**4**) ...... (fall) from the sky and crashing onto houses and cars. Rescue teams (**5**) ...... (not fly) because conditions were terrible. We were lucky – people (**6**) ...... (not climb) the volcano that day. But then I saw a helicopter ...

◯ **VOCABULARY · PAGE 125**

Listening

8 🎧 **Listen and then write sentences about the story in exercise 7. Use the words in the circles and the correct form of the past continuous.**

Two men were flying in a helicopter.

two men
the girl
the lava
the radio

fly
look for
shout
move
work

◯ **Finished?**

Make a list of movies about natural phenomena.
The Perfect Storm

A SHOCKING EXPERIENCE

Lightning usually strikes tall objects or metal. It also strikes about 2,500 people every year. A lot of those people, approximately 94%, survive their 100-million-volt experience. These are the stories of two lucky lightning survivors.

Steve Marshburn was working in an office. He was near a metal window when lightning struck it. The lightning also struck Steve. He wasn't touching the window, but he had a metal object in his hand. His colleagues were looking at him, but they didn't want to touch him because they were frightened.

Arnold Hanson, another victim, was walking in a field when lightning struck him. It lifted him 45cm in the air. His twelve-year-old son, Dale, saw the incident and helped Arnold.

The victims of lightning often have problems after their experience. Steve and Arnold can't remember things, and they find it difficult to sleep. Other victims never feel cold. Their advice? Don't stand near tall objects or metal, and don't walk or play sports in a storm!

Reading

1 Are the sentences true or false? Guess the answers.

1 Lightning sometimes strikes people.

2 Lightning can move objects.

3 People usually don't survive when lightning strikes them.

4 People feel normal after lightning strikes them.

5 Lightning strikes tall objects.

2 🎧 Read and listen to the text. Check your answers to exercise 1.

3 Read the text again and answer the questions.

1 Where was Steve Marshburn working when lightning struck him?

2 Was he touching the window?

3 Why didn't his colleagues help him?

4 Where was Arnold Hanson walking?

5 What problems do Steve and Arnold have?

Pronunciation

/ɪŋ/

4 🎧 Listen and repeat.

1 filming	4 working
2 moving	5 walking
3 raining	6 touching

5 🎧 Listen to the sentences. What verb forms do you hear? Choose a or b.

1	a	move	b	moving
2	a	touched	b	touching
3	a	play	b	playing
4	a	stand	b	standing

Exploring grammar

Past continuous: questions

6 Complete the chart with *was*, *were*, and *weren't*.

Questions	
Was I / he / she / it	walking?
(1) ...... we / you / they	talking?
Short answers	
Yes, I (2)	No, I **wasn't**.
Yes, we **were**.	No, we (3) ....

(**GRAMMAR · PAGE 118**)

7 Look at the picture. What was happening when lightning struck? Put the words in order. Then answer the questions.

in an office? / she / working / Was

Was she working in an office?

No, she wasn't.

1 Where / the farmer / working? / was
2 was / she / What / wearing?
3 Was / she / a hat? / wearing
4 Were / watching? / other people
5 What / doing? / were / the cows
6 the cows / Were / watching / the farmer?

8 Look at the pictures and the verbs. Write questions in the past continuous.

Were you having breakfast at eight o'clock this morning?

this morning   1 yesterday

2 last night   3 this morning

4 last Saturday   5 last night

Speaking

9 Ask and answer the questions from exercise 8.

Finished?

What were you and your family doing at midnight on New Year's Eve last year? Write sentences.

At nine o'clock we were having dinner.

Tornado

Listening

1 🎧 Guess the order of pictures a–e. Then listen and check.

2 🎧 Listen again and answer the questions.

1. Was Brad watching the TV when Jenny called?
2. What special program was on TV?
3. What was the advice of the TV reporter?
4. Where did Brad go on his bike?
5. Why was it difficult to bike?
6. Why were people running to their houses?
7. Where was Jenny's mother?
8. Where was the tornado moving?

Writing

A story: stages of writing

You are going to write a story for a newspaper.

3 Look at photos a–c and choose a topic. Think of a title.

4 Write answers to questions 1–12 for your story.

Paragraph 1

1 When did it happen?

2 Where were you?

3 Were you with other people?

4 What were you doing before it happened?

Paragraph 2

5 What were you doing when it started?

6 What were other people doing?

7 Was the situation frightening?

8 Why? / Why not?

9 What did you do?

Paragraph 3

10 What were people doing after this incident?

11 How did you feel?

12 What did you do?

5 Write a rough version of your story.

6 Check your rough version. Is it interesting? Are there any mistakes?

7 Write your final version.

Speaking

8 Read your story aloud to the class.

Finished?

Read another student's story.
Is their story interesting?
Are there any mistakes?

a earthquake

b volcano

c hurricane

Progress Check 4

Natural phenomena

1 **Write the words.**

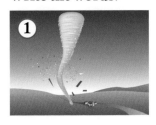

Verbs of movement

2 **Match the words in the box with pictures 1–6.**

> climb   crash   fly   move   fall   lift

Past continuous: affirmative and negative

3 **Complete the text with the correct form of the past continuous.**

I *was watching* (watch) TV last night when my friend called. I (**1**) ...... (watch) a program about the floods. Linda (**2**) ...... (sit) in a kayak. She (**3**) ...... (call) from a public phone near her house. She (**4**) ...... (not call) from home because there was one meter of water in her living room. Her mom and dad (**5**) ...... (stay) at a friend's house. Linda was in town with some other people from the kayak club. She (**6**) ...... (help) the police. They (**7**) ...... (not look) for people; they (**8**) ...... (look) for people's pets.

Past continuous: questions

4 **Put the words in order. Then look at exercise 3 and answer the questions.**

1 What / watching? / was / Linda's friend

2 in a helicopter? / Was / sitting / Linda

3 were / Where / her parents / staying?

4 helping / How / the police? / Linda / was

5 Were / people? / looking for / they

The World of English 2

Friends and Neighbors
(pages 44 and 45)

Review: **simple past and past continuous**

Function: **Asking for and giving advice**

1 What is Greg doing?

Culture File
(pages 46 and 47)

Topic: **Teenagers and money**

2 What are some popular part-time jobs for teenagers?

The World of Pop
(page 48)

Artist: **Travis**

Country: **Scotland**

Song: **Why does it always rain on me?**

3 What's the first line of the song?

Friends and Neighbors

Where's my wallet?

1

Greg	Nikki, can you lend me a dollar?
Nikki	Yes, there's some money in my bag. Here you go.
Luke	Nikki, are you playing tennis or what?
Nikki	Yes, I'm coming! Greg, do you want to play?
Greg	Uh, no thanks. I should go home. I need to study.

2

Luke	Look! Greg's playing those video games again. He should go home and study.
Nikki	Oh, yes. What should we do? What do you think, Luke?
Luke	I'm not sure. Maybe we should say something.
Nikki	Yes, you're right.

3

Waitress	That's five dollars, please.
Nikki	Hey! Where's my wallet?

4

Nikki	Luke, I can't find my wallet, and when I called Greg he ran away.
Luke	Maybe he didn't hear you. He was running for a bus.
Nikki	Or maybe he was trying to avoid me.
Luke	What are you saying, Nikki?
Nikki	Look, there he is. Hey, Greg, Greg! Come here!

5

Nikki	Now listen to me, Greg Brown ...
Waitress	Excuse me, I think this is your wallet. It was under your chair.
Nikki	Oh, thanks! How stupid! I'm really sorry, Greg.
Greg	What's the problem? Come on, let's walk home.

Reading

1 🎧 **Read and listen to Friends and Neighbors. Then answer the questions.**

1 Why didn't Greg play tennis?

2 Why were Luke and Nikki worried about Greg?

3 Why was Greg running?

4 Did Greg take Nikki's wallet?

5 Why does Nikki say she is sorry?

Useful expressions

2 **Find the expressions in the story. Then check their meaning.**

1 Here you go.   3 How stupid!

2 What should we do?   4 I'm really sorry.

Dialog

Asking for and giving advice

3 🎧 **Look at this extract from Friends and Neighbors. Listen and repeat. Concentrate on your rhythm and intonation.**

A: Look! Greg's playing those video games again. He should go home and study.

B: Oh, yes. What should we do? What do you think, Luke?

A: I'm not sure. Maybe we should say something.

B: Yes, you're right.

4 **Look at the pictures. What's the situation in each picture?**

5 **Practice a dialog in pairs. Change the blue words in the dialog in exercise 3. Use your ideas from exercise 4.**

Culture File 2

Teenagers and money

1 **Work in pairs. Discuss the questions.**

   1 How do you get money?

   2 What things do you buy?

2 **Guess the answers to questions 1–6. Then read and check your answers.**

   1 What percentage of American and British teenagers get an allowance?

   2 Is it legal for a fourteen-year-old to work in the U.S. and the U.K.?

   3 What are some typical part-time jobs for American and British teenagers?

   4 What four things do American or British teenagers usually spend their money on?

   5 What kinds of entertainment do teenagers spend their money on?

   6 What new thing do boys and girls spend money on?

Teenagers and money: a survey

About 75% of American and British teenagers get a regular allowance from their parents. A typical amount is $10 or £5 a week. They also get money from parents and relatives on holidays and on birthdays.

Some teenagers get money when they do chores, such as buying the groceries, washing the car, or cooking a meal.

Part-time jobs are also popular. In the U.S., during the school year, a fourteen-year-old can work eighteen hours a week, and a maximum of three hours a day. In the U.K., the figures are twelve hours a week but only two hours on a school day. When school is not in session, American fourteen-year-olds can work 40 hours a week, and a maximum of eight hours a day but British fourteen-year-olds can only work a maximum of 25 hours a week and a maximum of five hours a day.

Some popular part-time jobs in the U.S. and the U.K. are:
- paperboy or papergirl
- babysitter
- worker in a fast food restaurant
- supermarket stock boy or stock girl

Statistics show that young people spend their money on food, entertainment, clothes, and transportation. Those between the ages of ten and thirteen buy a lot of candy. Young people between the ages of fourteen and eighteen prefer fast food and soda. In the entertainment category, movies, DVDs, CDs, games, books, and magazines are all very popular.

Boys and girls buy different things. Boys buy more computer games and sports equipment. Girls buy more clothes, fashion accessories, presents, and cosmetics. Nowadays young people also spend a lot of money on cell phones and text messaging.

3 🎧 **Listen to Becky and Leo talking about money. Who is American and who is British? How did you know?**

4 🎧 **Listen again and choose the correct answer.**

Becky is . . .
a fifteen years old. b sixteen years old.

Leo is . . .
a fifteen years old. b sixteen years old.

1 Becky's allowance is . . .
a £6 a week.   b £5 a week.

2 Leo's allowance is
a $5 a week.   b $10 a week.

3 Becky spends money on . . .
a accessories.   b CDs and magazines.

4 Leo spends money on . . .
a movies, music, and computer games.
b books and magazines.

5 Becky bought a new . . .
a computer.   b cell phone.

6 Leo passed his
a lifeguard exams. b art exams.

7 Becky sometimes does . . .
a her homework. b chores.

8 Leo works in
a a supermarket.   b a movie theater.

9 Becky . . . saves money.
a always   b never

10 Leo . . . saves money.
a often   b never

5 **Who spends more money on things 1–5? Boys, girls, or both? Write B, G, B/G.**

1 make-up ......

2 computer games ......

3 sports equipment ......

4 clothes ......

5 texting ......

Project

Prepare a questionnaire to find out:
- how your classmates get their money
- what they spend it on
- if they save money

Find the results for boys and girls. Draw a bar chart to illustrate your results.

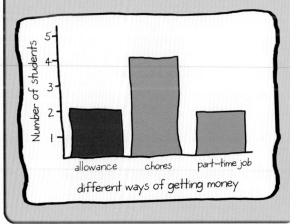

The World of Pop 2

Travis

Members: Francis Healy (vocals),
Neil Primrose (drums), Andy Dunlop (guitar),
and Douglas Payne (bass)

Formed: Glasgow, Scotland, 1990

Previous names: Glass onion, Red telephone box

First single: *All I Wanna Do Is Rock* (1996)

First top ten hit: *Why Does It Always Rain On Me?*
(1999)

History: Fran Healey's mother lent the band £600, and
they used the money to make a record. They sent it to
DJs and record companies.

Travis (Scotland)

**1 Read the information about Travis and
answer the questions.**

1 Who sings in the band?

2 Where did the band form?

3 What was the original name of the band?

4 When did Travis have their first hit?

5 What did Fran's mother lend the band?

**2 🎧 Complete the song with the words in the
box. Then listen and check.**

> go   lightning   seventeen   eyes   days
> cold   tonight

**3 How does the singer feel? Choose four
adjectives from the box.**

> happy   tired   unhappy   energetic
> lucky   optimistic   unlucky   pessimistic

Why Does It Always Rain On Me?

1 I can't sleep *tonight*.
2 Everybody's saying everything's all right,
3 Still I can't close my (**1**) ......
4 I'm seeing a tunnel at the end of all these lights.

(Chorus)
5 Sunny (**2**) ......,
6 Where have you gone?
7 I get the strangest feeling you belong,
8 Why does it always rain on me?
9 Is it because I lied when I was (**3**) ......?
10 Why does it always rain on me?
11 Even when the sun is shining,
12 I can't avoid the (**4**) ......
13 Oh, where did the blue skies (**5**) ......?
14 And why is it raining so?
15 It's so (**6**) ......

(Repeat verse)
(Repeat chorus)

16 Why does it always rain on me?
17 Why does it always rain on me?
18 Why does it always rain on me?
19 Why does it always rain on me?

Grammar

Unit 1

have

Affirmative	
I you	have
he she it	has
we you they	have

Negative	
I you	don't have
he she it	doesn't have
we you they	don't have

Questions

Do	I you	have ...?
Does	he she it	have ...?
Do	we you they	have ...?

Short answers

Affirmative			Negative		
Yes,	I you	do.	No,	I you	don't.
Yes,	he she it	does.	No,	he she it	doesn't.
Yes,	we you they	do.	No,	we you they	don't.

- **We use *have* to mean "possess".**
  I *have* a skateboard.
  He *doesn't have* a computer.
  How many computer games *do* they *have*?

- **We do not use *have* in short answers.**
  Do you have a tarantula?
  No, I *don't*. NOT: ~~No, I haven't.~~

Simple present

Affirmative	
I you	play
he she it	plays
we you they	play

Negative	
I you	don't play
he she it	doesn't play
we you they	don't play

don't = do not
doesn't = does not

Questions

Do	I you	play?
Does	he she it	play?
Do	we you they	play?

Short answers

Affirmative			Negative		
Yes,	I you	do.	No,	I you	don't.
Yes,	he she it	does.	No,	he she it	doesn't.
Yes,	we you they	do.	No,	we you they	don't.

- **We use the simple present to talk about habits and routines.**
  I *don't go out* a lot.
  How often *do you go* to bed after midnight?

Spelling: third person singular (affirmative)

- **We form the third person singular of the *simple present* by adding an *-s* to the base form.**
  make ➤ make*s*

- **If the verb ends in a consonant + -y, we change the -y to -i and add -es.**
  try ➤ tr*ies*

- **If the verb ends in -ch, -ss, -sh or -o, we add -es.**
  wash ➤ wash*es*
  go ➤ go*es*

Adverbs of frequency

0%	....➤	100%
never	not usually sometimes usually	always

- **We usually put adverbs of frequency before the main verb, but note that they go after the verb *be*.**
  He *always* makes his bed.
  He doesn't *usually* clean his room.
  She is *never* late.

- **You can also put *sometimes* at the beginning of the sentence.**
  Barry *sometimes* washes the dishes.
  Sometimes Barry washes the dishes.

Unit 2
Present continuous

Affirmative	
I	'm reading
you	're reading
he she it	's reading
we you they	're reading

'm = am
're = are
's = is

Negative	
I	'm not reading
you	aren't reading
he she it	isn't reading
we you they	aren't reading

'm = am
aren't = are not
isn't = is not

Questions

Am	I	reading?
Are	you	reading?
Is	he she it	reading?
Are	we you they	reading?

Short answers

Affirmative			Negative		
Yes,	I	am.	No,	I	'm not.
Yes,	you	are.	No,	you	aren't.
Yes,	he she it	is.	No,	he she it	isn't.
Yes,	we you they	are.	No,	we you they	aren't.

- **We use the *present continuous* to talk about something that is happening at the time of speaking.**
  She *is writing* a book.

- **We do not use the -ing form in short answers.**
  Are they *studying*?
  yes, they are.
  NOT: *yes, they are studying.*

Simple present and present continuous

- **We use the *simple present* to talk about habits and routines.**

- **We use the *present continuous* to talk about something that is happening at the time of speaking.**
  Mark usually *helps* Lucy with her homework, but today he *'s watching* a video.

Unit 3
Simple past: affirmative and negative

Affirmative		Negative	
I you he she it we you they	lived	I you he she it we you they	didn't live

didn't = did not

- **We use the *simple past* to talk about states and actions in the past.**

  Walt Disney *created* Mickey Mouse and Disneyland.

  In 1996 LeAnn Shannon *won* three gold medals.

Spelling: simple past regular verbs

- **We usually form the *simple past* with the base form of the verb + -ed.**

  help ➤ help*ed*   stay ➤ stay*ed*

- **If the verb ends in -e, we add -d.**

  create ➤ create*d*   use ➤ use*d*

- **If the verb ends in a consonant + -y, we change the -y to -i before adding -ed.**

  bury ➤ bur*ied*   study ➤ stud*ied*

- **If the verb ends in a vowel + a single consonant, we usually double the consonant before adding -ed.**

  stop ➤ stop*ped*

  One common exception is travel ➤ travel*ed*

Pronunciation: simple past endings

- **When the base form of the verb ends in /t/ or /d/, we pronounce the -ed ending /ɪd/.**

  invent*ed*, start*ed*

- **When the base form of the verb ends in a vowel or a voiced consonant, we pronounce the -ed ending /d/.**

  die*d*, argu*ed*

- **When the base form of the verb ends in a voiceless consonant, we pronounce the -ed ending /t/.**

  help*ed*, work*ed*

Simple past: irregular verbs

- **There are some irregular verbs that do not end in -ed in the simple past form.**

  win ➔ *won*   buy ➔ *bought*

  🔵 IRREGULAR VERBS · INSIDE BACK COVER

Simple past: questions

Questions		
Did	I you he she it we you they	win the prize?

Short answers					
Affirmative			**Negative**		
Yes,	I you he she it we you they	did.	No,	I you he she it we you they	didn't.

- **We form questions in the simple past with *did* + the base form.**

  Did you buy any presents?

  What *did you win*?

  NOT: ~~What *you won*?~~

  OR: ~~What *did you won*?~~

was / were

Affirmative

I	was
you	were
he she it	was
we you they	were

Negative

I	wasn't
you	weren't
he she it	wasn't
we you they	weren't

wasn't = was not
weren't = were not

Questions

Was	I ...?
Were	you ...?
Was	he ...? she ...? it ...?
Were	we ...? you ...? they ...?

Short answers

Affirmative			Negative		
Yes,	I	was.	No,	I	wasn't.
Yes,	you	were.	No,	you	weren't.
Yes,	he she it	was.	No,	he she it	wasn't.
Yes,	we you they	were.	No,	we you they	weren't.

- **We use *was* and *were* (the *simple past* forms of *be*) to talk about the state of things and people in the past.**

  The questions *were* difficult.

Unit 4
Past continuous

Affirmative

I	was sleeping
you	were sleeping
he she it	was sleeping
we you they	were sleeping

Negative

I	wasn't sleeping
you	weren't sleeping
he she it	wasn't sleeping
we you they	weren't sleeping

Questions

Was	I	sleeping ...?
Were	you	sleeping ...?
Was	he she it	sleeping ...?
Were	we you they	sleeping ...?

- **We use the *past continuous* to talk about something that was happening at a certain time in the past.**

  In 1992 *they were filming* in Hawaii.

Vocabulary

Unit 1

Activities
exercise /'ɛksərsaɪz/
go out /goʊ 'aʊt/
go shopping /goʊ 'ʃɑpɪŋ/
meet friends /mit 'frɛndz/
play computer games /pleɪ kəm'pyutər geimz/
play guitar /pleɪ gɪ'tar/
play sports /pleɪ 'spɔrts/
stay in /steɪ 'ɪn/
spend (time) /spɛnd (taɪm)/
surf the Internet /sərf ði 'ɪntərnɛt/
watch TV /watʃ ti 'vi/
sing /sɪŋ/
use a computer /yuz ə kəm'pyutər/

Jobs at home
clean your room /klin yər 'rum/
go shopping /goʊ 'ʃɑpɪŋ/
make dinner /meɪk 'dɪnər/
make your bed /meɪk yər 'bɛd/
take out the garbage /teɪk aʊt ðə 'garbɪdʒ/
wash the dishes /waʃ ðə 'dɪʃɪz/

Other nouns
attitude /'ætətud/
bar chart /'bar tʃart/
black belt /'blæk bɛlt/
boa /'boʊə/
computer game /kəm'pyutər geɪm/
hobby /'habi/
hour /'aʊər/
insect /'ɪnsɛkt/
life /laɪf/
martial art /marʃl 'art/
minute /'mɪnət/
movie theater /'muvi 'θiətər/
saint /seɪnt/
shopping mall /'ʃɑpɪŋ mɔl/
shower /'ʃaʊər/
skateboard /'skeɪtbɔrd/
South America /saʊθ ə'mɛrɪkə/
spider /'spaɪdər/
taekwondo /taɪ'kwandoʊ/
tarantula /tə'ræntʃələ/
week /wik/
weekend /wik'ɛnd/
worm /wərm/
year /yɪr/

Adjectives
different /'dɪfrənt/
free /fri/
interesting /'ɪntrəstɪŋ/
lazy /'leɪzi/
lucky /'lʌki/
tired /'taɪərd/

Other verbs
check /tʃɛk/
cook /kʊk/
copy /'kɑpi/
go rollerblading /goʊ 'roʊlərbleɪdɪŋ/
help /hɛlp/
practice /'præktəs/
remember /rɪ'mɛmbər/
sleep /slip/
study /'stʌdi/

Adverbs
a lot /ə 'lat/
also /'ɔlsoʊ/
approximately /ə'praksəmətli/
at home /ət 'hoʊm/
too /tu/

Unit 2

Forms of communication
alphabet /'ælfəbɛt/
Braille /breɪl/
cell phone /sɛl 'foʊn/
code /koʊd/
fax machine /'fæks məʃin/
hieroglyphics /haɪrə'glɪfɪks/
language /'læŋgwɪdʒ/
message /'mɛsɪdʒ/
(tele)phone /('tɛlə)foʊn/
sign /saɪn/
sign language /'saɪn læŋgwɪdʒ/
symbol /'sɪmbl/
text message /'tɛkst mɛsɪdʒ/
videophone /'vɪdioʊ foʊn/

Verbs for communicating
argue /'argyu/
call /kɔl/
chat /tʃæt/
e-mail /'imeɪl/
interrupt /ɪntə'rʌpt/
laugh /læf/
ring /rɪŋ/
send /sɛnd/
shout /ʃaʊt/
talk /tɔk/

Other nouns
anagram /'ænəgræm/
basketball score /'bæskətbɔl/
comic /'kɑmɪk/
extinction /ɪk'stɪŋkʃn/
finger /'fɪŋgər/
Indian /'ɪndiən/
machine /mə'ʃin/
Maori /'maʊri/
teenager /'tineɪdʒər/
textbook /'tɛkstbʊk/
tradition /trə'dɪʃn/
wrist /rɪst/

Countries
England /'ɪŋglənd/
Britain /'brɪtn/
Egypt /'idʒɪpt/
North America /nɔrθ ə'mɛrɪkə/
Northern Ireland /nɔrðərn 'aɪərlənd/
Republic of Ireland /rɪpʌblɪk əv 'aɪərlənd/
Scotland /'skɑtlənd/
Wales /weɪlz/

Languages
Arabic /'ærəbɪk/
Chinese /tʃaɪ'niz/
Choctaw /'tʃaktɑ/
Gaelic /'geɪlɪk/
Hindi /'hɪndi/
Spanish /'spænɪʃ/
Portuguese /pɔtʃə'giz/
Italian /ɪ'tæliən/
Welsh /wɛlʃ/

Other verbs
change /tʃeɪndʒ/
come in /kʌm 'ɪn/
communicate /kə'myunəkeɪt/
draw /drɔ/

preserve /prɪ'zərv/
say hello /seɪ he'loʊ/
say sorry /seɪ 'sari/
sit down /sɪt 'daʊn/

Adjectives
blind /blaɪnd/
Egyptian /ɪ'dʒɪpʃn/
late /leɪt/
official /ə'fɪʃl/
useful /'yusfl/

Punctuation
capital letter /kæpətl 'lɛtər/
period /'pɪriəd/

World of English 1

Useful expressions
Don't worry. /doʊnt 'wəri/
I'm in trouble. /aɪm ɪn 'trʌbl/
It's your fault. /ɪts 'yər fɔlt/
Let's make a deal. /lɛts meɪk ə 'dil/

Houses and homes
air-conditioning /'ɛə kəndɪʃnɪŋ/
apartment /ə'partmənt/
bungalow /'bʌŋgəloʊ/
cottage /'katɪdʒ/
downstairs /daʊn'stɛrz/
duplex /'duplɛks/
inherit /ɪn'hɛrɪt/
mansion /'mænʃn/
porch /pɔrtʃ/
rocking chair /'rakɪŋ tʃɛr/
single-family house /sɪŋgl fæmli 'haʊs/
upstairs /ʌp'stɛrz/

Unit 3

Prizes
ceremony /'sɛrəmoʊni/
certificate /sər'tɪfəkət/
check /tʃɛk/
cup /kʌp/
medal /'mɛdl/
Nobel Peace Prize /noʊbɛl 'pis praɪz/
trophy /'troʊfi/

Competitions
Cup Final /'kʌp faɪnl/
Grand Prix /grand 'pri/

Olympic Games /əlɪmpɪk ˈgeɪmz/
Paralympic Games /pærəlɪmpɪk ˈgeɪmz/
tournament /ˈtɜrnəmənt/
World Cup /wərld ˈkʌp/

Other nouns

autograph /ˈɔtəgræf/
bag /bæg/
beach volleyball /bitʃ ˈvɑlibɔl/
biography /baɪˈɑgrəfi/
boss /bɔs/
champion /ˈtʃæmpiən/
charity /tʃærəti/
competition /kɑmpəˈtɪʃn/
dollar /ˈdɑlər/
founder /ˈfaʊndər/
medallist /ˈmɛdəlɪst/
gymnasium /dʒɪmˈneɪziəm/
lottery ticket /ˈlɑtəri tɪkət/
match /mætʃ/
millionaire /mɪlyəˈnɛr/
nation /ˈneɪʃn/
pacifist /ˈpæsəfɪst/
poor /pʊr/
present /ˈprɛznt/
president /ˈprɛzədənt/
record /ˈrɛkərd/
rose /roʊz/
shopping list /ˈʃɑpɪŋ lɪst/
university /yunəˈvərsəti/
war /wɔr/
wife /waɪf/
winner /ˈwɪnər/
work /wərk/

Verbs

(be) born /(bɪ) ˈbɔrn/
buy /baɪ/
commemorate /kəˈmɛməreɪt/
create /kriˈeɪt/
die /daɪ/
forget /fərˈgɛt/
invite /ɪnˈvaɪt/
mail /meɪl/
prefer /prɪˈfər/
start /stɑrt/
stay /steɪ/
win /wɪn/
work /wərk/

Adjectives

gold /goʊld/
Olympic /əˈlɪmpɪk/

several /ˈsɛvrəl/
young /yʌŋ/

Time expressions

(three years) later /(θri yɪrz) ˈleɪtər/
after /ˈæftər/
in 1874 /ɪn eɪtin sɛvənti ˈfɔr/
then /ðɛn/
yesterday /ˈyɛstərdeɪ/

Adverb

both /boʊθ/

Unit 4

Natural phenomena

blizzard /ˈblɪzərd/
drought /draʊt/
earthquake /ˈərθkweɪk/
flood /flʌd/
hurricane /ˈhərəkən/
inferno /ɪnˈfərnoʊ/
lightning /ˈlaɪtnɪŋ/
storm /stɔrm/
tornado /tɔrˈneɪdoʊ/
volcano /vɑlˈkeɪnoʊ/

Verbs of movement

climb /klaɪm/
crash /kræʃ/
fall /fɔl/
fly /flaɪ/
lift /lɪft/
move /muv/
run /rʌn/
walk /wɔk/

Other nouns

advice /ədˈvaɪs/
agony /ˈægəni/
air /ɛr/
bike /ˈbaɪk/
cameraman /ˈkæmrəmæn/
cloud /klaʊd/
colleague /ˈkɑlig/
condition /kənˈdɪʃn/
cow /kaʊ/
crater /ˈkreɪtər/
engine /ˈɛndʒən/
experience /ɪkˈspɪriəns/
farmer /ˈfɑrmər/
field /fild/
gas /gæs/
helicopter /ˈhɛləkɑptər/
image /ˈɪmɪdʒ/

incident /ˈɪnsədənt/
kayak /ˈkaɪæk/
lava /ˈlɑvə/
object /ˈɑbdʒɛkt/
office /ˈɔfəs/
pilot /ˈpaɪlət/
police /pəˈlis/
rainwater /ˈreɪnwɔtər/
survivor /sərˈvaɪvər/
torture /ˈtɔrtʃər/
TV reporter /ti vi rɪˈpɔrtər/
victim /ˈvɪktɪm/
volt /voʊlt/
window /ˈwɪndoʊ/

Verbs

contact /ˈkɑntækt/
enjoy /ɪnˈdʒɔɪ/
erupt /ɪˈrʌpt/
escape /ɪˈskeɪp/
film /fɪlm/
happen /ˈhæpən/
rescue /ˈrɛskyu/
survive /sərˈvaɪv/
touch /tʌtʃ/

Adjectives

acidic /æˈsɪdɪk/
active /ˈæktɪv/
alive /əˈlaɪv/
cold /koʊld/
dangerous /ˈdeɪndʒərəs/
hot /hɑt/
metal /ˈmɛtl/
safe /seɪf/
sick /sɪk/
shocking /ˈʃɑkɪŋ/

World of English 2

Useful expressions

Here you go. /ˈhɪr yu goʊ/
How stupid! /haʊ ˈstupɪd/
I'm really sorry. /aɪm rili ˈsɑri/
What should we do? /wɑt ʃəd wi ˈdu/

Teenagers and money

accessory /ækˈsɛsəri/
allowance /əˈlaʊəns/
assistant /əˈsɪstənt/
babysitter /ˈbeɪbisɪtər/
chore /tʃɔr/
lifeguard /ˈlaɪfgɑrd/
make-up /ˈmeɪk ʌp/

paperboy/girl /ˈpeɪpərbɔɪ, -gərl/
part-time /pɑrt taɪm/
soft drink /sɔft ˈdrɪŋk/

Workbook Part A

Mick Gammidge
Ben Wetz

OXFORD

UNIVERSITY PRESS

1 ○ Time out

Vocabulary

Activities

1 Complete the puzzle. Use the names of the activities.

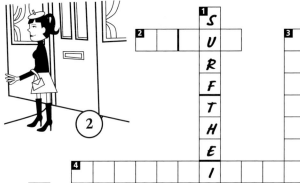

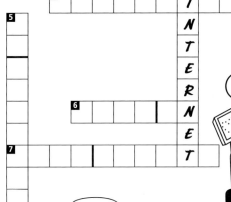

The crossword spells: S U R F T H E I N T E R N E T

Look!

have

2 Complete the sentences with the correct form of *have*.

Mel **has** a camera. (✔)

You **don't have** a skateboard. (✗)

1 I .... a blue T-shirt. (✔)

2 Chris .... a bike. (✗)

3 My parents .... a car. (✔)

4 We .... a computer in the classroom. (✗)

Exploring grammar

Simple present

3 Complete the sentences. Use the affirmative forms of the verbs in parentheses.

Amanda

Mike

Amanda **plays** (play) table tennis.

1 Amanda .... (like) art.

2 Mike .... (surf) the Internet.

3 He .... (practice) on his skateboard a lot.

4 They .... (play) sports.

4

4 Complete the sentences. Use the affirmative and negative forms of the verbs in parentheses.

They **don't use** (not use) computers to do homework.

1 Amanda .... (not watch) TV in her room.

2 Amanda .... (play) soccer.

3 Mike .... (like) tennis.

4 Mike .... (not read) magazines in his room.

5 They .... (not play) the guitar.

5 Complete the text. Use the verbs in parentheses.

Amanda and Mike are friends. On weekends, they **don't stay** (not stay) in a lot. They (**1**) .... (go out) and they (**2**) .... (meet) friends.

Every week they (**3**) .... (go) to the sports club. Amanda is good at table tennis.

Mike (**4**) .... (not like) table tennis because he (**5**) .... (not win) when he (**6**) .... (play) with Amanda!

6 Helen visits her grandfather every year. Complete the questions with *Do* or *Does*. Then answer the questions.

Grandfather's house in Canada

Does she visit her grandfather in Mexico? **No, she doesn't.**

1 .... they swim in the ocean?

....

2 .... they go on camping trips?

....

3 .... Helen's grandfather like art?

....

4 .... Helen go to the movies?

....

Vocabulary

Jobs at home

1 Complete the expressions for jobs at home. Use the words in the box.

> your room   the dishes   your bed
> dinner   the garbage   shopping

clean **your room**

1 make ....

2 go ....

3 wash ....

4 make ....

5 take out ....

Look!

like / don't like + -ing

2 Look at the information about Tina and write sentences. Use *like* and *doesn't like + -ing*.

~~clean her room~~ (✗)	watch TV (✓)
stay in on Fridays (✗)	get up late (✓)
do homework (✗)	play sports (✓)

She doesn't like cleaning her room.

1 ....

2 ....

3 ....

4 ....

5 ....

Look!

Spelling rules: third person -*s*

3 Complete the chart. Use the third person singular form of the verbs in the box.

> ~~love~~   watch   go   make   study
> listen   wash   marry   try

Rules	Examples
most verbs: add -*s*	*loves*, ..., ...
verbs ending in consonant + *y*: change -*y* to -*i* and add -*es*	.........., ..., ...
verbs ending in -*ch*, -*ss* or -*o*: add -*es*	.........., ..., ...

Exploring grammar
Adverbs of frequency

4 Write the adverbs in the correct order in the chart.

> not usually ~~always~~ sometimes never usually

always
1 ....
2 ....
3 ....
4 ....

5 Cross out the extra adverb in each sentence.

Martina always goes ~~always~~ shopping on weekends.

1 Never Martina never drinks coffee for breakfast.

2 She doesn't usually make usually dinner.

3 She sometimes washes sometimes the dishes.

4 She usually watches TV after usually school.

5 Her father sometimes helps sometimes her with her homework.

6 Martina always makes her bed in the morning always.

6 Answer the questions about you.

> How often do you go to school in the summer?
>
> ***I never go to school in the summer.***

1 How often do you see your grandparents on weekends?

....

2 How often do you go to the movies?

....

3 How often do you go to parties?

....

4 How often do you dance at parties?

....

5 How often do you make your bed?

....

7 Complete the questions about you. Use *How often ...?* and *do* or *does*. Then answer the questions.

> ***How often do*** you get up late on Sundays?
>
> ***I always get up late on Sundays.***

1 .... you get a good grade for your homework?

....

2 .... you stay in on Saturday nights?

....

3 .... you practice English with your friends?

....

4 .... your father cook dinner?

....

Reading

1 **Read the texts. Are the sentences true or false?**

Peter has a bike. ***True.***

1 Peter can't swim. ....

2 Peter can speak some Spanish. ....

3 Sue gets up late on Saturday mornings. ....

4 Sue and Julia like the Internet. ....

5 Sue sometimes goes out on Sunday evenings. ....

2 **Now read the texts again and answer these questions.**

What is Peter's favorite town?
Orleans is his favorite town.

1 What does Peter always do in Orleans?

....

2 Where does Peter go on vacation with his family?

....

3 How long do he and his family go on vacation for?

....

4 What does Peter like doing in Mexico?

....

5 What is Sue's best friend's name?

....

6 Why do they go to the nightclub?

....

7 What does Sue do on Sunday nights?

....

8 Does Sue go to bed late on Sundays?

....

Orleans, Cape Cod

My school vacations

In the school vacations I like traveling to interesting places. Sometimes my friends and I bike out of the city, and we go camping. We also visit other towns. My favorite place is Orleans on Cape Cod. It's by the ocean, and it has a great beach. The ocean is sometimes really cold, but we always go swimming!

I also go on vacations with my family. We usually spend a week or two in Mexico, and I practice my Spanish. It's really fun, but I can't understand everything people say. I love shopping in Mexico, and I always buy presents for my friends. I usually buy them something unusual.

My weekends

Sue

I always get up early on Saturdays because I like weekends. I usually meet my best friend, Julia, and we play computer games. We also surf the Internet. You can find information about everything on the Internet. It's amazing!

We sometimes go out to the nightclub on Saturday nights. We're crazy about music, and we also love dancing. I always stay in on Sunday nights and do my homework. After that, I watch my favorite music program on TV, but I don't go to bed late — school starts early on Monday morning.

Writing

Writing about free time: *also*, *and*, and *but*

3 Circle *also* in the texts about Peter and Sue.

Is it before or after the verb? ....

4 **Choose the correct word in the sentences.**

Ben likes listening to pop music. He **also** / **but** loves dancing.

1 He speaks English. He **and** / **also** goes to Chinese classes.

2 Ben likes making dinner for his family, **but** / **also** he hates washing the dishes.

3 On Sundays, he plays computer games. He **also** / **and** surfs the Internet.

4 Ben studies music **also** / **and** he plays the guitar.

5 Write about your free time. Remember to use *also*, *and*, and *but*.

<u>My free time</u>

....

....

....

....

....

....

....

....

....

....

....

....

....

....

Look!

Big numbers

6 **Write the correct numbers.**

| one thousand | one hundred |
| one million | five hundred thousand |

500 + 500	= **one thousand**
1 500,450 + 499,550 =	....
2 630 + 370	= ....
3 57 + 43	= ....
4 322,700 + 177,300 =	....

2 ○ Communicate

Vocabulary

Forms of communication

1 Match the parts. Then write the words.

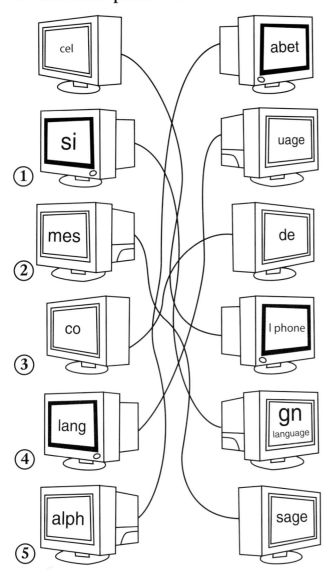

cell phone

1 ....
2 ....
3 ....
4 ....
5 ....

Exploring grammar

Present continuous

2 Complete the sentences. Use the present continuous form of the verbs in parentheses.

Carla**'s calling** (call) her friend, Patsy.

1 They .... (go) to the movies.

2 Carla .... (not eat).

3 They .... (watch) a horror movie.

4 Patsy .... (not have) a good time.

3 Complete the sentences. Use the present continuous form of the verbs in parentheses.

She**'s listening** (listen) to music, but she **isn't dancing** (dance).

1 The teacher .... (speak), but they .... (not listen).

2 They .... (use) computers, but they .... (not surf) the Internet.

3 She .... (stay in), but she .... (not do) her homework.

4 Todd .... (play) tennis, but he .... (not win).

4 Complete the dialog. Use the present continuous form of the verbs in parentheses.

Tom: Hi, Mark. What **are** you **doing** (do)?

(**1**) .... you

.... (watch) TV?

Mark: No, I'm not. Why?

Tom: *Code busters* is on. It

(**2**) .... (start) now.

Mark: I can't watch it.

I (**3**) .... (finish) my history project right now.

Tom: The project! It's really difficult, and you're terrible at history. Who

(**4**) .... (help) you?

Mark: No one! I don't need any help.

Tom: I (**5**) .... (not do) it now. I (**6**) .... (watch) *Code busters* now.

Mark: OK, tell me about the program later. Bye.

Vocabulary

Verbs for communicating

1 Find seven more verbs.

```
S  H  O  G  E  U  I
P  I  A  T  A  K  N
E  -  M  A  I  L  T
S  H  C  A  L  L  E
T  O  R  L  E  N  R
A  C  H  A  T  T  R
L  A  G  U  E  S  U
K  A  R  G  U  E  P
I  N  S  H  O  U  T
```

e-mail

1 ....

2 ....

3 ....

4 ....

5 ....

6 ....

7 ....

Exploring grammar

Simple present and present continuous

2 Complete the table with examples a–d and meanings e–h.

Examples:

a We watch TV.

b We're watching TV.

c I'm not drinking coffee.

d I don't drink coffee.

Meanings:

e never

f sometimes or usually

g right now

h not right now

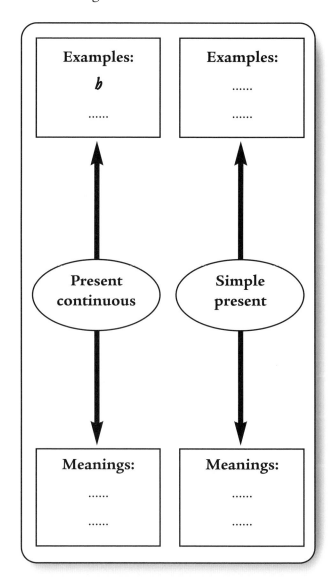

3 Look at the picture of Miguel and circle the correct form of the verb.

He **(speaks)** / **is speaking** English.

1 He **watches** / **is watching** TV right now.

2 He **listens** / **is listening** to CDs every day.

3 Miguel **sits** / **is sitting** down right now.

4 He **doesn't write** / **isn't writing** to his friend right now.

4 Answer the questions about you.

1 Do you sleep at night?
Yes, I do.

2 Are you sleeping right now?
....

3 Do you eat chocolate every day?
....

4 Are you eating chocolate right now?
....

5 Are you celebrating your birthday today?
....

6 Do you celebrate your birthday every year?
....

5 Complete Miguel's letter. Use the simple present or present continuous form of the verbs in the box.

write go swim send not like listen

Dear Sam,

I'm writing to give you my new address.
I (**1**) .... you a photo
of our new house. It's great. We
(**2**) .... to the beach
every day, and I (**3**) ....
in the ocean every afternoon.
I (**4**) .... to some
fantastic music right now. It's by an
American pop group, Green Day. Usually,
I (**5**) .... American
music, but this is really good.
Best wishes,
Miguel

Reading

1 **Read the e-mail and complete the chart.**

From:	Gisela Encinas	Date:	Friday, December 5th
To:	International Friends' Club	Subject:	e-mail friends

Hi!

My name is Gisela. I'm from Cali in Colombia. I speak Spanish, and I'm learning English. I want to learn English because all my favorite pop songs are in English. English is also good for traveling because a lot of people speak English all around the world.

Did you know that more than 60 countries use English as an official language? More than 75% of the world's letters are in English. I always write to Eri, my Japanese pen pal, in English because she is also learning English at school. We write in English because I can't speak Japanese, and she can't speak Spanish.

There's a lot of English on the Internet too. Did you know that approximately 80% of the information on computers is in English? And 60% of phone calls are also in English.

English has a lot of words from other languages. For example "guitar" comes from the Spanish word, "guitarra". A lot of other languages use English words too. My friend Eri says that a lot of Japanese words come from English, but they have a different pronunciation in Japanese. Eri uses the word "sandoichi", for example. It means "sandwich"!

Gisela

Countries with English as an official language:	*More than 60%*
Letters in English:	
Phone calls in English:	
Information on computers in English:	

2 **Read the e-mail again and answer the questions.**

Where is Gisela from?

She's from Cali in Colombia.

1 Why does Gisela want to learn English?

....

2 Where is Eri from?

....

3 What language is Eri learning at school?

....

4 What is the Japanese word for "sandwich"?

....

Look!

Countries and nationalities

3 Complete the chart.

Country	Nationality
Spain	*Spanish*
France	(1) ....
Argentina	(2) ....
Japan	(3) ....
Australia	(4) ....
Italy	(5) ....
China	(6) ....
Brazil	(7) ....
Poland	(8) ....

Writing

An essay: periods and capital letters

4 Rewrite the paragraph with periods and capital letters.

> american english and british english are different they have different sounds and there are many different words some of the grammar rules are different too

American English and ....

....

....

....

....

....

....

5 Answer the questions about you.

1 Do you have any pen pals?

....

2 Do you write letters in English?

....

3 Do you play computer games in English?

....

4 Do you read in English on the Internet?

....

5 Do you read comics or magazines in English?

....

6 Do you listen to English music?

....

6 Use your answers from exercise 5 to write a paragraph about you. Use the e-mail in exercise 1 to help you.

English is important to me because ....

....

....

....

....

....

....

....

....

....

....

....

....

Exploring grammar

Simple present

1 Put the words in the correct order.

Roxy   Rick

music. / study / Rick and Roxy
Rick and Roxy study music.

1 Roxy / in a / plays / rock group.

....

2 a lot. / stay in / Rick and Roxy / don't

....

3 dancing / love / at the nightclub. / They

....

4 goes / on Saturdays. / shopping / Roxy

....

5 doesn't / Rick / shopping. / like

....

2 Complete the questions. Then write answers.

play   listen   dance   play   like

Does Roxy **play** in a rock group?
Yes, she does.

1 .... Roxy .... the drums?

....

2 .... Rick .... to Roxy's group?

....

3 .... Rick and Roxy ....?

....

4 .... they .... classical music?

....

Adverbs of frequency

3 Circle the correct adverbs of frequency. Then rewrite the sentences with the correct adverbs.

I copy my friend's homework. (always / (never))

I never copy my friend's homework.

1 Good students listen to their teacher. (always / never)

....

2 People wash the dishes after dinner. (usually / never)

....

3 Vegetarians eat meat. (often / never)

....

4 Good soccer players practice a lot. (always / never)

....

Present continuous

4 Complete the sentences. Use the present continuous form of the verbs in parentheses.

Affirmative
She*'s listening* (listen) to a CD.
1 They .... (study) math.

Negative
2 She .... (listen) to a CD.
3 They .... (study) math.

Questions
4 What .... she .... (listen) to?
5 .... they .... (study) English?

Simple present and present continuous

5 Complete the text. Use the present continuous or simple present form of the verbs in the box.

~~go shopping~~   argue   ask
go   talk   love   buy

Today, Carla*'s going shopping*. It's Patsy's birthday today. Carla is Patsy's best friend. Carla (**1**) .... a present for Patsy. She's in a bookstore, and she (**2**) .... to the sales clerk. Carla (**3**) .... the sales clerk about books about Hollywood. Carla and Patsy (**4**) .... to the movies every weekend, but they sometimes (**5**) .... about which movie to see. The problem is that Carla (**6**) .... horror movies, but Patsy doesn't!

Vocabulary

Activities

1 Find five more activities.

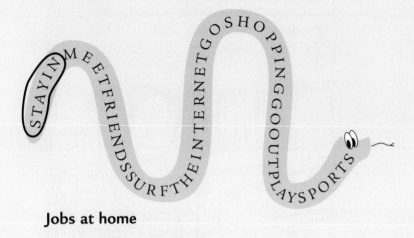

STAYIN M EETFRIENDSSURFTHEINTERNETGOSHOPPINGGOOUTPLAYSPORTS

Jobs at home

2 Complete the words.

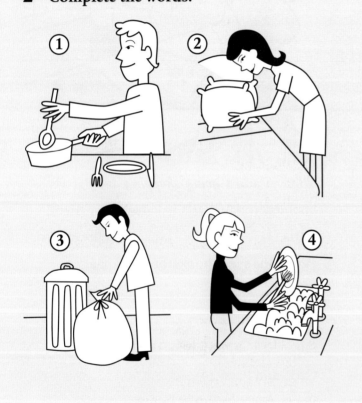

1 m_ _ _ _ d_ _ _ _ _ _ _

2 m_ _ _ _ y_ _ _ _ b_ _ _

3 t_ _ _ _ o_ _ t_ _ g_ _ _ _ _ _ _

4 w_ _ _ _ t_ _ d_ _ _ _ _ _

Forms of communication

3 Complete the words.

We communicate information to other people in a | m | **e** | s | s | **a** | **g** | e | .

1 We use a c | | d | | to send a secret message.

2 French is a l | | n | | u | | g | | , and English is too.

3 A s | | g | | usually communicates an idea without language.

4 The English a | | p | | a | | e | | has 26 letters.

Verbs for communicating

4 Complete the puzzle.

| | | I | N | T | E | R | R | U | P | T | | |

Useful expressions

5 Complete the dialog with the expressions.

> Let's make a deal.   ~~I'm kind of busy.~~
> Don't worry.   It's your fault.

Jen:	Sue, I need your advice.
Sue:	OK, but *I'm kind of busy* right now.
Jen:	But my brother wants his CD and I don't have it. (**1**) .... You broke it!
Sue:	(**2**) .... Everything will be OK. He doesn't know what happened to his CD.
Jen:	He really hates me borrowing things.
Sue:	Don't tell him! (**3**) .... I'll buy him a new CD. OK?

Dialog

Making requests

6 Look at the pictures and write requests.

open / door

1 clean / room

2 look for / dog

3 take out / garbage

Can you open the door, please?

1 ....

2 ....

3 ....

Culture File

7 Circle the correct answers in the quiz.

1 A duplex is ...
a the only house on the street.
b one of a pair of houses. *(circled)*
c an old stone house.

2 A single-family house is ...
a a house on one floor.
b a set of rooms in a tall building.
c separate from other houses.

3 A cottage is ...
a a large modern house.
b a small house in the country for weekends or vacations.
c a new detached house.

4 A house that is on one floor is a ...
a single-family house.
b mansion.
c bungalow.

5 How big is a mansion?
a Small.
b Large.
c Very large.

6 What type of home is usually in a tall building?
a A bungalow.
b An apartment.
c A cottage.

7 Which type of house is usually the most expensive?
a A mansion.
b A duplex.
c A bungalow.

8 Which type of home doesn't usually have a garden?
a An apartment.
b A single-family house.
c A cottage.

3 ⬤ Prizes

Vocabulary

Prizes

1 Find four more prizes.

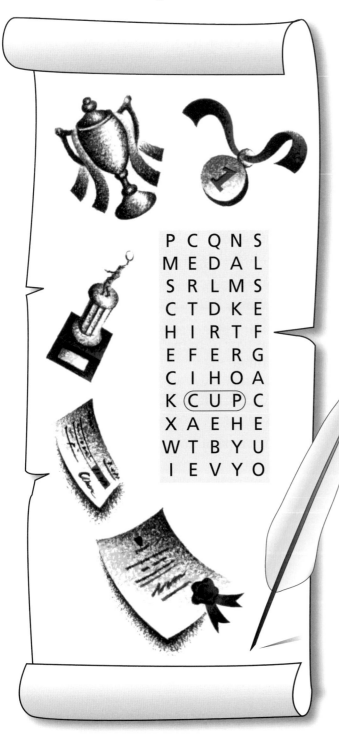

```
P C Q N S S
M E D A L L
S R L M S S
C T D K E E
H I R T F F
E F E R G G
C I H O A A
K C U P C C
X A E H E E
W T B Y U U
I E V Y O O
```

Irregular verbs

2 Match the infinitives with the simple past forms.

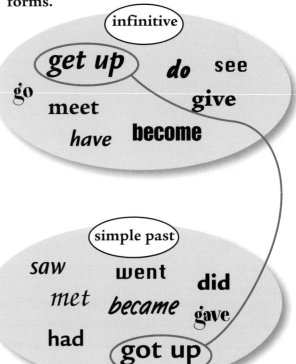

infinitive

get up **do** see

go **give**

meet

have **become**

simple past

saw went **did**

met **became** gave

had **got up**

Exploring grammar

Simple past: affirmative and negative

3 Circle the simple past forms in the sentences.

Marco Polo went to China in 1292.

1 They gave Madame Curie the Nobel Prize in 1911.

2 Columbus didn't discover Australia.

3 Stephen Hawking wrote *A Brief History of Time* in 1988.

4 Brazil didn't win the World Cup in 2006.

5 Valentina Tereshkova became the first woman in space in 1963.

4 Complete the sentences. Use the simple past form of the verbs in the box.

~~not get up~~   buy   not stay   have   talk

Gina *didn't get up* late.

1 She .... a shower.

2 She .... at home.

3 She .... a new shirt.

4 She .... to her friend.

5 Complete the dialog. Use the simple past form of the verbs in parentheses.

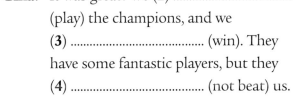

Gina: I *had* (have) my first important basketball game yesterday. I
(**1**) .... (buy) a new shirt and some sneakers for it.

Ken: Was it a good game?

Gina: It was great! We (**2**) ....
(play) the champions, and we
(**3**) .... (win). They have some fantastic players, but they
(**4**) .... (not beat) us.

Ken: Awesome! I'm sorry that I
(**5**) .... (not go) to the game.

Gina: All my friends (**6**) ....
(go) to the game because my father
(**7**) .... (give) everyone tickets! After the game, we
(**8**) .... (have) a big party, and we all (**9**) ....
(celebrate). We (**10**) ....
(not stop) until really late!

Exploring grammar
Simple past questions

Last summer, my family won a travel competition. The prize was a vacation to Brittany in France. We went for two weeks, and our hotel was really big. It was great! Brittany was awesome.

We were on the plane for hours. At first it was exciting, but then it became boring. My sister and I read a book about France.

I tried to speak French in Brittany. It was fun. We practiced saying "Bonjour" — it's French for "Hello" — and asking for things in French. It was really difficult because we don't study French at school. We only study Spanish.

1 Read about Zoe and answer the questions.

Did Zoe's family go on vacation?
Yes, they did.

1 Did they go to Spain?

....

2 Did Zoe like the vacation?

....

3 Did they go by ship?

....

4 Did they stay in a hotel?

....

2 Now complete these questions about Zoe's vacation. Use the verbs in the box. Then write the answers.

> ~~win~~   go   like   speak   read

Did Zoe's family ***win*** a competition?
Yes, they did.

1 .... Zoe's family .... to Spain for two weeks?

....

2 .... Zoe and her sister .... a book about France?

....

3 .... Zoe .... Spanish on vacation?

....

4 .... she .... Brittany?

....

3 Put the words in the correct order. Use the answers to help you.

go / Where / last Saturday? / you / did

Where did you go last Saturday?

I went to London.

1 Who / you / go with? / did

....

I went with my parents.

2 What / see? / you / did

....

We saw Trafalgar Square and Big Ben.

3 do? / What / you / did

....

We went to a soccer game.

4 buy / Did / any presents? / you

....

Yes, I did. I bought this soccer scarf.

was / were

4 Complete the dialog. Use *was, wasn't, were,* and *weren't.*

Steve:	Where ***were*** you last week?
Andy:	I (**1**) .... on vacation in Florida.
Steve:	(**2**) .... it fun?
Andy:	Yes, it (**3**) .... great!
Steve:	How many days (**4**) .... you there for?
Andy:	We (**5**) .... there for two weeks.
Steve:	(**6**) .... you in a hotel?
Andy:	No, we (**7**) .... We (**8**) .... with my grandparents. They live in Miami.
Steve:	(**9**) .... the weather good?
Andy:	No, it (**10**) .... It rained!

Reading

1 Read about Stephen Hawking. Put the pictures in the correct order.

1 *d*   2 ...   3 ...   4 ...

(a)

(b)

(c) Cambridge

(d) Oxford

2 Read the text again and answer the questions about Stephen Hawking.

What does Stephen Hawking do?
He's a scientist.

1 What did he study at university?

....

2 When did he become ill?

....

3 What does he use to help him with his illness?

....

4 What happened in 1981?

....

5 Was his first book popular?

....

6 Did the book sell in more than one country?

....

STEPHEN HAWKING'S UNIVERSE

Stephen Hawking was born in 1942. He is a world famous scientist and an expert on space and time. Stephen is trying to find the answers to some very big questions, such as: How did the universe begin? How will it end?

Stephen was a student at Oxford University. He studied math and science. Then, in 1962, he became very ill. He was only twenty-one years old, but the doctors said he had only two more years to live. The doctors were wrong – he didn't die. He can't walk now, but he uses a wheelchair. He talks with the help of a computer.

After Oxford, Stephen went to Cambridge University. Three years later, in 1965, he became a Doctor of Philosophy.

Because of his health problems, it was difficult for him draw diagrams or to write. So he started to think in pictures. With this new way of thinking, he became one of the most famous scientists in the world. In 1981, he met the Pope in Rome. They talked about his ideas. Then, in 1988, he wrote his first important book, *A Brief History of Time*. It sold over 9 million copies in 33 different languages.

Writing

A biography: time expressions

3 Complete the sentences from the text in exercise 1. Use the time expressions in the box.

> ~~after~~   then   later   then

After Oxford, Stephen went to Cambridge University.

1 ...., in 1962, he became very ill.

2 Three years ...., in 1965, he became a Doctor of Philosophy.

3 ...., in 1988, he wrote his first important book.

4 Read the sentences about Marie Curie. Put the sentences in order.

1 *c*   2 ...   3 ...   4 ...   5 ...   6 ...   7 ...

a She died in 1934 from exposure to radiation.

b In 1906, Pierre Curie died in a street accident.

c Marie Curie and her husband devoted their lives to science and radioactivity.

d She won the Nobel Prize for Chemistry in 1911. She was the first person to win two Nobel prizes.

e In 1903, they won the Nobel Prize for Physics.

f In 1935, Marie and Pierre's daughter, Irène, won the Nobel Prize for Chemistry.

g In 1906, she took her husband's job at the Sorbonne in Paris. She was the first woman to teach at the famous university in 650 years!

5 Write about Marie Curie. Use the sentences in exercise 4 and the time expressions in exercise 3.

> *Women in Science:*
> *Marie Curie (1867–1934)*
>
> *Marie Curie and her husband devoted their lives to science.* ....

Le Petit Parisien

4 ● The elements

Vocabulary

Natural phenomena

1 Read the clues and complete the puzzle.

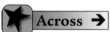 **Across →**

2 Wind and snow.
3 Everything moves, and houses fall down.
5 Wind and rain.
6 Hot lava!
8 It comes from the sky in storms.
9 There isn't any rain.

 **Down ↓**

1 A strange wind, common in the U.S.
4 A very big and dangerous storm.
7 After a lot of rain.

Verbs: movement

2 Complete the sentences with the verbs in the box.

| fly | lift | move | crash | climb | fall |

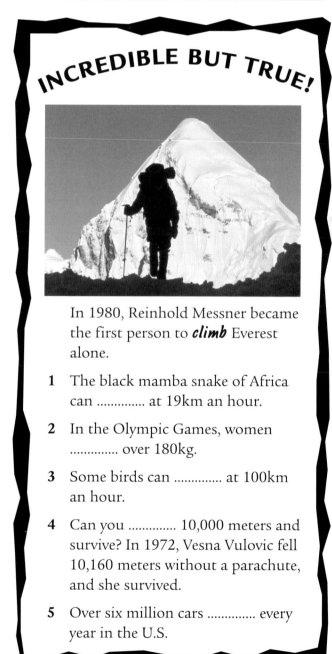

INCREDIBLE BUT TRUE!

In 1980, Reinhold Messner became the first person to *climb* Everest alone.

1 The black mamba snake of Africa can .... at 19km an hour.

2 In the Olympic Games, women .... over 180kg.

3 Some birds can .... at 100km an hour.

4 Can you .... 10,000 meters and survive? In 1972, Vesna Vulovic fell 10,160 meters without a parachute, and she survived.

5 Over six million cars .... every year in the U.S.

Exploring grammar

Past continuous: affirmative and negative

3 Look at the picture and complete the sentences. Use the past continuous form of the verbs in the box.

> read go play stand talk listen climb

Tina **was going** to the library.

1 Bill .... a magazine.

2 Alex and Alice .... to the band.

3 Pam .... to Bill.

4 The musicians .... music in the park.

5 Bill and Pam .... under a tree.

6 The cat .... the tree.

4 Complete Lucy's letter with the past continuous form of the verbs in parentheses.

TEENAGE MAGAZINE
YOUR LETTERS

Dear Teenage Magazine,

One Saturday last winter, my dad **was watching** (watch) the weather news on TV. There was a terrible blizzard in Canada. I (**1**) .... (not listen) to it really, but then I remembered my friend Jill and her family. They (**2**) .... (learn) to snowboard that weekend – in Canada!

I tried to call Jill on her cell phone about twenty times, but I (**3**) .... (not get) an answer. I (**4**) .... (become) really worried. Finally, I called their hotel, and Jill was safe.

She and her family (**5**) .... (not practice) in the dangerous blizzard. They (**6**) .... (sit) in front of a warm fire, and they (**7**) .... (drink) hot chocolate. Jill (**8**) .... (not answer) her cell phone because she didn't have it with her. It was at home. She forgot it!

Lucy (14), St. Louis

Exploring grammar

Past continuous: questions

1 Complete the questions about Claire's trip to Peru. Use the past continuous.

TV Monday

20:00 Volcano!
A report from Claire Ward in Peru.

Claire and her camera team / film / the volcano on Wednesday afternoon?

Were Claire and her camera team filming the volcano on Wednesday afternoon?

1 they / travel / on Monday morning?

....

2 Claire / travel / on Tuesday afternoon?

....

3 Claire / interview / the victims on Friday morning?

....

4 Claire and her team / fly / home on Saturday evening?

....

5 Claire / work / on Sunday?

....

2 Now look at Claire's day planner and write short answers to the questions in exercise 1.

Monday	Thursday
flew to Peru with camera team 1:00 p.m. – arrived in Peru 11:00 p.m.	all day – interviewed victims
Tuesday	**Friday**
traveled to volcano by car 10:30 a.m. – arrived 6:00 p.m.	all day – interviewed victims
Wednesday	**Saturday**
filmed volcano 10:00 a.m. – 10:00 p.m.	in car 7:30 a.m. – 5:00 p.m. flew home 6:30 p.m.
	Sunday
	slept!

Yes, they were.

1 ....

2 ....

3 ....

4 ....

5 ....

3 Answer the questions about you. Use the past continuous.

What were you doing at nine o'clock last night?
I was having dinner with my family.

1 What were you doing at eight o'clock this morning?

....

2 What was your family doing on Saturday?

....

3 What were you doing at four o'clock yesterday?

....

4 What were your classmates doing this morning?

....

4 Complete the police officer's questions to Mr. Ford. Use the past continuous of the verbs in the box.

> sit   go   fly   travel   do   plan

Officer:	Where **were** you **going**?
Mr. Ford:	To London, Heathrow.
Officer:	What time (**1**) .... you .... to arrive?
Mr. Ford:	About three o'clock.
Officer:	Who (**2**) .... the helicopter?
Mr. Ford:	Mrs. Walsh was the pilot.
Officer:	How many people (**3**) .... in the helicopter?
Mr. Ford:	There were two of us.
Officer:	Where (**4**) .... you ....?
Mr. Ford:	Behind the pilot.
Officer:	What (**5**) .... you ....?
Mr. Ford:	I was working.

5 Complete the interview. Use the past continuous form of the verbs in parentheses.

Reporter:	Mr. Ford, **were** you **traveling** (travel) in the helicopter?
Mr. Ford:	Yes, I was.
Reporter:	It was a very violent storm. (**1**) .... you .... (watch) the storm from the helicopter?
Mr. Ford:	No. I (**2**) .... (work). I (**3**) .... (write) a letter. Then suddenly – BANG! The lightning struck the helicopter, and it started to fall.
Reporter:	What (**4**) .... the pilot .... (do)?
Mr. Ford:	She (**5**) .... (fight) with the controls, and she (**6**) .... (shout) into her radio!
Reporter:	What (**7**) .... you .... (think) about?
Mr. Ford:	I (**8**) .... (not think) about anything. But I was very frightened.
Reporter:	And how do you feel now?
Mr. Ford:	Lucky to be alive!

Our Lucky Escape!

Last March, the weather was really rainy. One afternoon, I was sitting in Dean's living room. Dean and I were listening to music and playing computer games.

We were talking about the terrible weather, and Dean's mom was watching the storm. Then suddenly it happened! The music stopped, the computer stopped working, and we were sitting in the dark! We looked through the window, and we saw that there were no lights in any of the houses on the street. Then water started coming under the door and into the house! It was a flood! Soon there were about fifty centimeters of water in the room. And it wasn't stopping! We were cold and wet, and we were feeling a bit frightened. Dean's family lives under mine, so Dean, his mom, and I ran up the stairs to my house.

When the rain stopped, there were two meters of water in the street. Our moms were talking about what to do, and then we heard someone shouting to us. My dad and another man were in a boat! He was there to rescue us. We all felt really happy to see him. We climbed through the window and into the boat. Soon we were in my grandfather's house, safe and warm again!

Reading

1 **Read Leila's story and answer the questions.**

1 Were Leila and Dean frightened when the flood started?

....

2 Are Leila and Dean neighbors?

....

3 Who rescued them?

....

4 How many meters of water were there in the street when Leila's dad arrived?

....

5 Where did they go after the flood?

....

Writing

A story: stages of writing

2 **Imagine you are Leila or Dean. Look at the questions and underline the information in Leila's story.**

Paragraph 1

1 When did it happen?

2 Where were you?

3 What were you doing before it happened?

Paragraph 2

4 What were you doing when it started?

5 Was the situation frightening?

6 Why? / Why not?

7 What did you do?

Paragraph 3

8 What were people doing after this incident?

9 How did you feel?

10 What did you do?

3 Imagine you are one of the people in the picture story. Think about answers to the questions in exercise 2 and make notes.

....

Paragraph 1 ....

....

....

....

Paragraph 2 ....

....

....

....

Paragraph 3 ....

....

....

....

....

4 Write a neat version of your story.

Review: Units 3 and 4

Exploring grammar

Simple past: affirmative and negative

1 Complete the sentences about Pat. Use the simple past form of the verbs in the box.

> go ~~buy~~ enjoy not come not stay
> not travel win

Pat **bought** a lottery ticket.

1 She .... a lot of money.

2 Pat .... at home.

3 She .... on vacation with her friends.

4 They .... by plane.

5 They .... home for a month.

6 Pat really .... it.

Simple past: questions

2 Complete the dialog. Use the simple past form of the verbs in parentheses.

TV1: You **won** (win) the lottery two months ago. What
(**1**) .... you
.... (do) first?

Pat: I (**2**) .... (call) my friend, and she
(**3**) ....
(not believe) me!

TV1: What (**4**) .... you
.... (do) with the money?
What (**5**) .... you
.... (buy)?

Pat : I (**6**) .... (buy) presents for all my friends. Then I went on vacation.

TV1: Where (**7**) .... you
.... (go)?

Pat : To the Caribbean.

TV1: Who (**8**) .... you
.... (go) with?

Pat : I went with all my friends!

was / were

3 **Circle the correct form of the verb.**

Pat (was) / were very lucky.

1 Her numbers **was / were** the winning numbers.

2 Her vacation **was / were** great fun.

3 It **was / were** a month long.

4 It **was / were** sunny every day.

5 Her friends **was / were** happy.

6 She **was / were** on the NYTV1 show.

Past continuous: affirmative and negative

4 **Complete the text. Use the past continuous form of the verbs in the box.**

> watch ~~study~~ film not think
> become relax not go

Mount St. Helens, U.S.

Mount St. Helens became active again in March 1980. Experts **were studying** the volcano from a distance. They knew that it
(**1**) .... more active. They
(**2**) .... near it because it was very dangerous, but they
(**3**) .... the volcano from the air. People around the world
(**4**) .... the news about it on TV. One Sunday morning in May that year, CNN news reporter Jack Hamann
(**5**) .... at home. He
(**6**) .... about Mount St. Helens, but at about 8:30, he felt it erupt – over 150km away!

Past continuous: questions

5 **Complete the dialog. Use the past continuous form of the verbs in parentheses and short answers.**

A: Were any people **living** (live) near Mount St. Helens when it erupted?

B: Yes, they **were**. A lot of people moved away, but some stayed.

1 **A:** .... a plane .... (fly) over the volcano when it erupted?

B: Yes, it .... Two experts were studying the volcano from the air at the time.

2 **A:** .... people .... (visit) the area on camping trips at the time?

B: Yes, they .... Gary Rosenquist and his friends were there. They were lucky; they survived.

3 **A:** .... Jack Hamann .... (watch) Mount St. Helens when it erupted?

B: No, he .... He was reading the Sunday newspaper.

4 **A:** .... you .... (live) in the U.S. when the volcano erupted?

B: No, I .... I watched it on TV.

Vocabulary

Prizes

1 Find four more prizes.

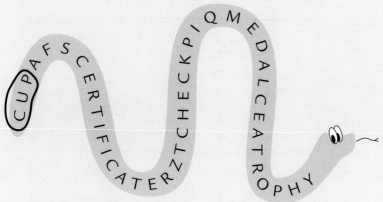

Irregular verbs

2 Find four more infinitives and their irregular simple past forms.

A	B	Q	A	C	B	P	D	R	N	I
U	V	U	B	W	E	J	T	Q	W	N
D	H	G	E	T	U	P	R	I	T	E
L	F	A	C	B	R	L	I	Z	K	N
M	E	E	O	B	G	O	T	U	P	E
Y	W	E	M	S	B	P	E	N	I	F
A	M	E	E	T	E	D	I	D	E	G
I	M	S	W	Y	C	O	K	A	M	A
W	O	S	R	Q	A	M	E	T	I	V
I	G	P	T	Z	M	Y	G	R	Y	E
J	Z	W	T	U	E	R	A	Z	E	P
F	G	I	V	E	I	D	S	E	M	L

become **became**

1 do ....

2 get up ....

3 meet ....

4 give ....

Natural phenomena

3 Match the parts of the words.

tornado

1 v.........................
2 b.........................
3 e.........................

4 s.........................
5 l.........................
6 h.........................
7 f.........................

Verbs: movement

4 Read the clues and write the verbs.

 **Across** →

1 Most birds can ... , but penguins can't!

3 My neighbors are really dangerous in their car. They ... it every week!

4 Be careful on the stairs. Don't ...!

5 Some people watch TV every evening. They sit on the sofa and they never ...!

 **Down** ↓

2 This backpack weighs about 100 kilos. I can't ... it!

3 Our cat can ... trees like a monkey!

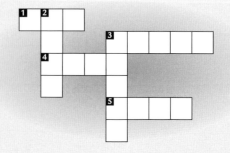

Useful expressions

5 Match expressions 1–4 with pictures
a–d.

1 I'm really sorry. **b**

2 Here you go. ....

3 What should we do? ....

4 How stupid! ....

Dialog

Asking for and giving advice

6 Complete the questions. Use the words
in the box. Then complete the advice.

(club/ join)
A: **What club should I join** at school?
B: **Maybe you should join** the movie club.

1 (present / buy)

A: .... Dan for his birthday?

B: .... him a book.

2 (clothes / wear)

A: .... for the nightclub?

B: .... your new shirt.

3 (food / cook)

A: .... for their dinner?

B: .... a pizza.

Culture File

7 Circle the correct answers in the quiz.

1 How many American teenagers get a
regular allowance from their parents?
a 65% (**b** 75%) **c** 85%

2 How much is a typical allowance?
a £5 or $10 a week.
b £10 or $20 a week.
c £15 or $30 a week.

3 How many hours a week can American
teenagers work when school is in session?
a Eighteen. **b** Seventeen.
c Nineteen.

4 How many hours a week can British
teenagers work when school is in session?
a Fifteen. **b** Twelve. **c** Nineteen.

5 How many hours can American
teenagers work on a school day?
a Two. **b** Three. **c** Four.

6 How many hours can British teenagers
work on a school day?
a Two. **b** Three. **c** Four.

7 When school is not in session, how many
hours a week can American teenagers
work?
a 20. **b** 30. **c** 40.

8 When school is not in session, how many
hours a week can British teenagers work?
a 15. **b** 25. **c** 35.

9 Which job is NOT a popular part-time
job in the U.S.?
a Babysitter.
b Worker in a fast food restaurant.
c Model.

10 What do American teenagers usually
spend their money on?
a Movies, CDs, clothes.
b Books, vacations, cars.
c Cell phones, cosmetics, furniture.

Irregular verbs

Infinitive	Simple past	Past participle
be /bi/	was, were /wəz/, /wər/	been /bin/
become /bɪkʌm/	became /bɪˈkeɪm/	become /bɪˈkʌm/
break /breɪk/	broke /broʊk/	broken /ˈbroʊkən/
bring /brɪŋ/	brought /brɔt/	brought /brɔt/
buy /baɪ/	bought /bɔt/	bought /bɔt/
can /kæn, kən/	could /kʊd/, /kəd/	–
come /kʌm/	came /keɪm/	come /kʌm/
cost /kɔst/	cost /kɔst/	cost /kɔst/
do /du/	did /dɪd/	done /dʌn/
draw /drɔ/	drew /dru/	drawn /drɔn/
drink /drɪŋk/	drank /dræŋk/	drunk /drʌŋk/
drive /draɪv/	drove /droʊv/	driven /ˈdrɪvən/
eat /it/	ate /eɪt/	eaten /ˈitən/
fall /fɔl/	fell /fɛl/	fallen /ˈfɔlən/
find /faɪnd/	found /faʊnd/	found /faʊnd/
fly /flaɪ/	flew /flu/	flown /floʊn/
forget /fərˈgɛt/	forgot /fərˈgɑt/	forgotten /fərˈgɑtən/
get /gɛt/	got /gɑt/	gotten /gɑtən/
get up /gɛt ˈəp/	got up /gɑt ˈəp/	got up /gɑt ˈəp/
give /gɪv/	gave /geɪv/	given /ˈgɪvən/
go /goʊ/	went /wɛnt/	been, gone /bin/, /gɔn/
grow /groʊ/	grew /gru/	grown /groʊn/
have /hæv/	had /hæd/	had /hæd/
hear /hɪr/	heard /hərd/	heard /hərd/
hit /hɪt/	hit /hɪt/	hit /hɪt/
keep /kip/	kept /kɛpt/	kept /kɛpt/
know /noʊ/	knew /nu/	known /noʊn/
leave /liv/	left /lɛft/	left /lɛft/
lose /luz/	lost /lɔst/	lost /lɔst/
make /meɪk/	made /meɪd/	made /meɪd/
mean /min/	meant /mɛnt/	met /mɛt/
meet /mit/	met /mɛt/	meant /mɛnt/
put /pʊt/	put /pʊt/	put /pʊt/
read /rid/	read /rɛd/	read /rɛd/
run /rʌn/	ran /ræn/	run /rʌn/
say /seɪ/	said /sɛd/	said /sɛd/
see /si/	saw /sɔ/	seen /sin/
sell /sɛl/	sold /soʊld/	sold /soʊld/
send /sɛnd/	sent /sɛnt/	sent /sɛnt/
sing /sɪŋ/	sang /sæŋ/	sung /sæŋ/
sleep /slip/	slept /slɛpt/	slept /slɛpt/
speak /spik/	spoke /spoʊk/	spoken /ˈspoʊkən/
spend /spɛnd/	spent /spɛnt/	spent /spɛnt/
swim /swɪm/	swam /swæm/	swum /swʌm/
take /teɪk/	took /tʊk/	taken /ˈteɪkən/
teach /titʃ/	taught /tɔt/	taught /tɔt/
tell /tɛl/	told /toʊld/	told /toʊld/
think /θɪŋk/	thought /θɔt/	thought /θɔt/
throw /θroʊ/	threw /θru/	thrown /θroʊn/
wake up /weɪk ˈəp/	woke up /woʊk ˈəp/	woken up /ˈwoʊkən ˈəp/
wear /wɛr/	wore /wɔr/	worn /wɔrn/
win /wɪn/	won /wʌn/	won /wʌn/
write /raɪt/	wrote /roʊt/	written /ˈrɪtən/